Bitty
From
Ashes

―❧―

DONIELLE MCCRAW

ISBN 978-1-63903-249-5 (paperback)
ISBN 978-1-63903-250-1 (digital)

Christian Faith Publishing, Inc.
832 Park Avenue
Meadville, PA 16335
www.christianfaithpublishing.com

Printed in the United States of America

This book is dedicated to the army that's rising up, my grandparents—who walked roads that helped get me here, and my family and friends—who were a special part of the journey that made me become Bitty from Ashes.

My husband, my leader, my partner, and best friend,
Tyler

My sons, my forever babies, men after God's own heart,
Mason and Ty Majer
(You're both my favorite.)

My mama, my shoulder to cry on, a courageous woman of God,
Memory

My daddy, my rock,
Donald

My stepdad, the warrior,
Clea

My sister, who I look up to,
Shanna

My mother-in-law, the overcomer,
Suzie

The couple that never stops teaching me,
Troy and Amy

Linda R., Cindy K., Amie W., Patty C.,
Cindy W., Krystal D., Brandi H.,
Candice A., Misty D., Angel B., David B., C. A.
Farmer, Gay Lynn J., and my church family

Thank you all for your love, support, and prayers.

July 10, 2020

Your victory is in your pen.
It always has been.
Keep writing, I am with you.
Fear not... For I am with you.
You know what to write.
It's in your heart...

I love you,
Husband

The Lord gave me this word for you.

07/10/20

YOUR VICTORY IS IN YOUR PEN.
IT ALLWAYS HAS BEEN.
KEEP WRITING, I AM WITH YOU.
FEAR NOT... FOR I AM WITH YOU
YOU KNOW WHAT TO WRITE.
IT'S IN YOUR HEART......

            I LOVE YOU,
                HUSBAND

THE LORD GAVE ME THIS WORD
FOR YOU.

INTRODUCTION

It has often been said that there are three sides to every story: your side, my side, and the truth.

Satan loves to twist truths and cause confusion in any situation, but he targets God-fearing marriages and families. His main goal is to separate you, and he's good at what he does. He's good at making us believe we're right and all others are wrong. If we let our guard down, he steals our focus. When our focus is away from God but on ourselves, we can begin to fall for Satan's tricks and schemes, leading us to have tunnel vision—a dark tunnel vision at that. Eventually, the enemy can completely blind us to anything or anyone in the light, even our spouse.

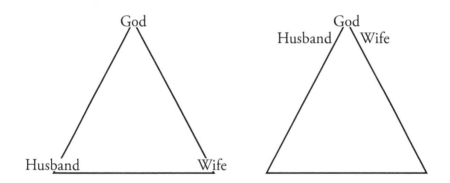

The closer we are to God, the closer we are to our spouse. The further we are from God, the further we are from our spouse.

Walk with me while I go through twenty-two years of how I became who I am today.

The first few chapters will quickly explain my life while the rest of the book proves that "your side, my side, and the truth," is Satan's way of separating us from God personally and in our marriages.

This is more than just a book about my life, more than a testimony about how our God is *the* God of the impossible, and more than proof of God restoring a broken marriage. It's a workbook, a journal, and a journey for you and me—all in one.

WHO AM I?

My name is Donielle ReShea McCraw (a.k.a. Bitty).

I am a sinner saved by grace that needs God every day.

I am a mistake maker who starts over every day.

I am forgiven!

I am not perfect, but I'm not expected to be.

I am clay, and God is my potter.

I am not defined by my mistakes.

I am bad in my flesh, but I'm *oh so* good in the spirit.

I am a woman who was lost but was sought out and found by the one true king. He left the ninety-nine to find me more times than I can count.

I am called.

I am blessed!

I am enough!

I am a work in progress.

If only you knew how big of a deal all of this is for me to say, I have always expected perfection from myself *until now*.

If you're not in a time of desperation for God and you're not 100 percent committed to healing and/or getting closer to God, then it's possible this book isn't for you. It will take time. You must be willing to open up and admit things to yourself and God, even if it hurts or makes you realize things you otherwise wouldn't have.

Before you sit down to begin reading, go ahead and get a pen or pencil, your Bible, markers or colored pencils, and your phone or tablet.

As the introduction says, this is more than a book. This is a way to study, learn, and retain information in ways that might seem a little different to some. When God asked me to be His hands and write this book, He gave me every detail, including all the different ways we learn and how this book should cover them all. Along with many other things, you will see drawn pictures throughout the book. I am a visual learner, so if I draw or see a picture, I stand a much better chance at remembering what the Lord has done for me, what He's teaching me, and the learned lessons that He wants me to remember. So before you decide not to participate in this area or any other area of the book, try it at least one time and see what it does for you.

After searching yourself and asking God to reveal it to you, write who you are. Be truthful with yourself. Be sure you don't accidentally put who you want to be. Put who you truly are.

On another sheet of paper or notebook, you can certainly put who you want to be.

WHO ARE YOU?

_____

_____

_____

_____

_____

_____

_____

_____

_____

_____

_____

_____

_____

_____

_____

_____

_____

_____

_____

_____

_____

_____

_____

_____

_____

_____

_____

Please pray before and after each chapter that you will be able to see and hear God!

CHAPTER 1

When God Ran

I was a fifteen-year-old girl who only attended church when it was convenient for me. I had gotten my driver's license four and a half months prior to the church service that changed two destinies.

It was a Wednesday night, and I just so happened to invite my fourteen-year-old cousin Stephanie to go with me. As we sat in the youth service, we both began to feel God knocking on our hearts. A dear lady named Gay Lynn, who was as godly as I feel you can get, spoke to all of us that night, telling us the prophetic dream the Lord had woken her up with that same week.

She told us all what God had told her. "There have been several wrecks lately and everyone has walked away without a scratch, but that is going to change. Someone that is in this room tonight will have a wreck." She continued by asking us all to come to the altar and make sure our lives and hearts belonged to God. She repeatedly told us she wasn't trying to scare us but that this was from the Lord, and she couldn't disobey by keeping it to herself.

I, just like everyone else I'm sure, thought it might be me, so I rushed to the altar. Stephanie, my cousin, did the same. In fact, she gave her heart to God that very night. As most teenagers do, at times,

I forgot the words we had been given almost immediately after we left church that night.

Friday, March 6, 1998, I woke up, got dressed, and left home excited because spring break would begin after this last day of school. I picked up Stephanie, and we headed out. When school was over, we left with unexpected, heavy rain falling. Stephanie and I drove around not knowing what was to come. I didn't know I wouldn't remember anything past leaving the school that day for the rest of my life, and Stephanie didn't know that she would go to her eternal destination that day. But one curve, two cars, and some rainfall changed both of our lives forever.

Stephanie, just days after giving her heart to Him, met Jesus on Friday, March 6, 1998. She went to the place we all long to be, but I went by ambulance to two hospitals without a scratch on me, or so they thought. Eight hours of two surgeries, a broken pelvis in five places, a broken tailbone in five places, a broken arm and collarbone, a weight drilled into my knee to pull my hips back in place, two weeks of memory loss, three months of no walking, a wheelchair, a walker, crutches, physical therapy, many doctors' visits, five screws and one plate, lots of prayer that the doctor wouldn't touch a single nerve and cause me to never walk again, missing the rest of my ninth-grade school year, being told I probably wouldn't have babies naturally because my pelvis couldn't spread enough, and many blood transfusions later—I became the girl/woman that Satan was determined would be bound. Guilt, shame, and depression for driving the car that tore my aunt and uncle's whole world apart for the rest of my life was the enemy's plan. I was a grief-stricken teen for what I had done to my cousin.

Satan had won. I was bound, just as he had planned, for thirteen years. Even though I served God, I knowingly and unknowingly faced battle after battle of fighting the enemy for my life. I had no peace, limited joy, more guilt and shame than imaginable, and happiness never lasted more than a couple of days at a time. I was a prisoner to depression. I was a prisoner to the lies, twisted truths, and tricks of Lucifer and all his demons.

But then, the king of glory rescued me! He sent not one but three people to intervene. I was fully healed from depression through the prayer of my husband in October of 2011. So many things that the enemy had stolen was taken back that day. Because Stephanie met Jesus the day my depression began, as I grew more and more in the Lord, I began to smile because God does not make mistakes. Stephanie, born on September 21, 1983, gave her life to God on March 4, 1998, and met her Savior two days later, March 6, 1998.

Are you bound by a circumstance in your life? Sometimes, we don't even realize we are bound. Ask God to help you see. Learn to hear His voice. Find the good in that circumstance and allow God to do a work in you.

Look up and write what this passage of scripture says about God helping you see (John 9:35–41).

_____

_____

_____

Write what it says about hearing His voice (John 9:35–41).

_____

_____

Look deeply at verse 37. The man who was no longer blind also heard Jesus speaking to him.

Your circumstance.

_____

_____

_____

_____

_____

_____

The good in that circumstance.

_____

_____

_____

_____

_____

_____

Are you bound by it in any way? Yes or no?
Pray circles around it and let God begin to heal you.

Draw a small picture that represents the circumstance in the box below.

Remember what the doctor told me would *probably* happen after the car wreck?

Mason Peace McCraw, March 23, 2004; Ty Majer McCraw, March 3, 2006—my two sons *both were born through natural birth.* Yep, I pushed both of those babies out!

CHAPTER 2

—ɯ—

The Sacrifice

I was a seventeen-year-old girl cleaning our house for my aunt's traditional visit from Arkansas for Christmas. It was December 17, 1999, when I got a phone call from someone frantically asking to speak to my dad. I watched his face turn to terror as he dropped the phone and screamed, "Let's go!"

Donald Justin Pugh (a.k.a. Justie)—son, brother, friend, God chaser, witness, the glue that held our family together, who was kind to everyone; a prayer warrior, a football player, a leader, who was loved by all; popular, straight-A college student, never missed church, prayed for his family, a Bible-studying servant like no other, who never met a stranger, a school-assembly-leading, life-loving, eighteen-year-old guy whom I am so privileged to get to call my brother—had lost his life in a hunting accident. The safety feature on the gun had failed to do its job. Again, there I was, one year and nine months after my first loss, facing it all over again. There was one thing different this time. I watched my own parents suffer. The glue that held our family together was gone.

Let's pause for just a minute and look up a scripture and write it below.

John 15:13

_____

_____

_____

The loss of such a perfect brother definitely contributed to those thirteen years of depression. At times, I would ask God why it was *the good child* and not me. Why take him and spare me? Here's the answer to that question. During my brother's graveside service, I knelt down beside his casket and gave my life to God. You see, he was ready, but I was not. Justie (Justin) was the wisest person I've ever known.

Each year, the youth at church wrote goal letters in January. Our youth pastor kept them until the next January, then gave them back to the writers.

Take a minute to read Justin's letter from January 1999 then go back to John 15:13 and read it again.

Goals

Listed below are four areas of your life. Write
out a goal in each area for 1999.
BE SPECIFIC AND HONEST

GOD: I would like to see myself mature in my relationship
with God. I would like to start studying my Bible
so that I will be ready to witness at anytime.

FAMILY: I want to show my family how serious I am about
Christ. Not only that but also lead each one of them to Christ
this year. I want to stand strong around them and be all I can
be for them. I will see my mom and dad saved again before

I die, even if it takes dying for them. I love them so much. I also want to tell my mom and dad I love them every day.

FRIENDS: I want to be more caring for my friends. In that, I will care about their eternity. I want to witness to them every day if that's what it takes.

SCHOOL/WORK: I want to go to school strictly for my education and occupational preferences. I also want to be a witness on my school campus in college.

Justin Pugh #55

GOALS

Listed below are 4 areas of your life. Write out a goal in each area for 1999
BE SPECIFIC & HONEST

GOD: _I would like to see my self mature in my relationship with God I would like to start studying my bible so that I will be ready to witness at anytime._

FAMILY: _I want to show my family how serious I am about Christ Not only that, but lead each one of them to christ this year I want to stand strong around them, and be all I can be for them. I will see my mom and dad once again before I die. Even if it takes dying for them. I love them so much. I also want to tell my mom + dad I love them everyday._

FRIENDS: _I want to be more caring for my friends, in that I will care about their eternity. I want to witness to them everyday if that's what it takes._

SCHOOL / WORK: _I want to go to school strictly for my education & occupational preferences I also want to be a witness on my school campus in College._

My brother Justin Pugh read and studied his Bible more times than I can count, yet John 15:13 was the one and only verse highlighted in his Bible. He led three hundred kids to the Lord on December 14, 1999, at a school assembly, and three days later, he gave up his life for his family. I have eternal life because he gave up his. When I was healed from depression in October of 2011, I began to *see* how good our God is through this tragedy as well as the tragedy in the last chapter. Why? Because I was able to *see*!

Please go to Bitty from Ashes (YouTube channel) and watch "Justin Pugh School Assembly 1999." Then come back. Please don't skip this video!

Study about love in John 15:1–17. Write what it tells you below. Pray to receive the wisdom of the Word before you begin reading.

_____

_____

_____

_____

_____

_____

_____

_____

_____

You cannot love others if you don't love yourself. You cannot love yourself if you do not love God. You cannot love God if you don't know God because God *is* love!

Read 1 Corinthians 13 and write down what love is.

_____

_____

_____

_____

_____

_____

_____

_____

_____

_____

_____

_____

_____

Write the definition of each one in the longer blanks below.

_____ __ __
_____ __ __
_____ __ __
_____ __ __
_____ __ __
_____ __ __
_____ __ __
_____ __ __
_____ __ __
_____ __ __
_____ __ __
_____ __ __
_____ __ __
_____ __ __

How well do you love according to God's definition? Rate yourself 1–10 in the first blank next to the definition. Leave the second blank for later.

CHAPTER 3

The Healing

For all of you who are wondering why or how I could live for God, have a wonderful husband, and two perfectly healthy sons yet still be depressed, there are two reasons. Let's look at this scripture.

James 1:2–8 NIV says,

> Consider it pure joy, my brothers, whenever you face trials of many kinds, because you know that the testing of your faith develops perseverance. Perseverance must finish its work so that you may be mature and complete, not lacking anything. If any of you lacks wisdom, he should ask God, who gives generously to all without finding fault, and it will be given to him. But when he asks, he must believe and not doubt, because he who doubts is like a wave of the sea, blown and tossed by the wind. That man should not think he will receive anything from the Lord; he is a double minded man, unstable in all he does.

Reason 1: This passage says "lacking nothing." I was still lacking in my relationship with God.

Reason 2: I wouldn't be able to be here helping you today if I had not gone through that time of depression.

God allows things to happen that fulfill His plan.

Now I don't know just how spiritual you have to be to believe what I'm about to tell you, but my mind isn't creative enough to make this up. I have found scripture to back it up, so don't close this book thinking I must be crazy. Trust me, I'm no more excited to write about this than you will be to hear/read it, but disobeying God by not writing it just isn't an option. It must be told!

I was a twenty-eight-year-old woman when the healing began. Depression had overwhelmed me to the point of finally listening.

Go back to chapter 1 and read the last paragraph one more time. It says God sent three people to intervene. Do you remember Gay Lynn? We had lost touch for a while, but God sent her to me *again*! Why? Because she was a willing vessel. She introduced me to a workbook that God had an aunt send to me two weeks later.

The two ladies have never met. My Aunt Cindy lives in Arkansas and Gay Lynn in Mississippi. I knew that workbook must be the key to my healing, so I began working on it immediately. My burden of depression seemed to get a little lighter yet still very present. It inspired me, so I began to pray and listen to God more. Because I was on my knees in prayer one night and God spoke to me, I went to my aunt and uncle, Stephanie's parents, after thirteen long years and was able to face them for the first time. I told them how sorry I was that we lost Stephanie in that tragic car wreck, and it was good. We all cried together, and I began to feel a little lighter burden on my shoulders.

Here's the part that will probably be hard to understand, but study it for yourself and you'll see just how real it is. It all started on a weekend marriage retreat at the beach with our church. Let me just throw in that my favorite person in all of creation (my husband) loves—and I do mean loves—one or one hundred tattoos. When he mentioned getting one during our free time at the retreat, I wasn't surprised at all. What did come as a surprise though was his tattoo of choice this time. This man of mine wanted an entire chapter out of the Bible on his back.

> The Lord is my shepherd, I shall not be in want. He makes me to lie down in green pastures, he leads me beside quiet waters, he restores my soul. He guides me in paths of righteousness for his name sake. Even though I walk through the valley of the shadow of death, I will fear no evil, for you are with me; your rod and your staff, they comfort me. You prepare a table before me in the presence of my enemies. You anoint my head with oil; my cup overflows. Surely goodness and love will follow me all the days of my life, and I will dwell in the house of the Lord forever. (Psalm 23 NIV)

My response, of course, was shock, but even more than the shock of so much writing, I didn't understand why that particular scripture. I even asked him why that one, but he never gave me an answer. I was thankful when he agreed to join my side of the argument without arguing and not get the tattoo. I don't remember now what we did instead of going to get a tattoo, but I'm sure it was something fun and a lot less painful.

On the way home from a weekend neither of us will ever forget, I was an emotional wreck to say the least. I was blessed from the experience of the retreat; sad because the next day my best friend and partner would be leaving me and our two sons, just like he did every two weeks to go offshore again, and I was pretty mad that was the life we had chosen. But for some reason, I just couldn't control my own feelings and actions. No matter how much my sweet Tyler tried to comfort me, it just seemed to make me angrier. I couldn't make it stop. Finally, Tyler found a place he could stop, and he pulled the car over into some gravel in the front of an old, seemingly abandoned, creepy-looking house. As I stared out the window with my arms crossed, I felt my husband, my love, my partner, my Tyler put his hand on my arm and tug a little, while, asking me to look at him, but I couldn't. No, I mean I literally couldn't. So I said, "I can't!"

Like anyone would, he asked why not, and my response was one that I as a Christian woman never thought I'd say, "Because of a demon!"

There were gourds hanging on the front porch of that old creepy house. I saw demonic faces on them. I don't know why or how, but that was God's way of revealing my demonic oppression to me. I felt that spirit stronger than anything I've ever felt before, but I will spare you the details of how.

The moment I said those four words, "Because of a demon," I began to feel and hear the authority my husband had over it. He began praying in his heavenly language, yet I understood what God was saying through him.

That had never happened before and it has never happened again, but this is what God said, "You are healed. That spirit is no longer with you. Now open the door and let it out so that it can go into that house with the rest of them."

The moment I cracked the car door open, Tyler's prayer stopped. He removed his hand from my arm, and a peace like no other entered my mind and my entire body. I looked at my husband as I trembled with a little bit of embarrassment but mainly relief. It was silent. I had no words at all, just peace. When Tyler said, "God has been preparing me for this for three weeks now. He didn't tell me exactly what, but He told me I'd have authority," I fell in love with my hubby all over again.

As we drove away from that old house where I had left my burdens and my depression for good, I told Tyler to find a field. I didn't know why, but I just felt such a strong urge and a pull to find a beautiful green field. After several miles, we found the field and pulled over. We simply rested in the presence of the Lord in the beautiful sunshine, laying on the green grass in the middle of nowhere.

For the first time in years, I actually heard the birds singing, and I noticed God's beautiful creations like never before. That, my friends, is what true peace feels like. After a little while of holding hands and laying quietly on the ground, Tyler whispered, "Does Psalm 23 make more sense to you now? This is why I wanted it tattooed on my back," and he quoted as much of the chapter as he could.

We walked through the valley of the shadow of death, and my husband did not fear the evil. He took authority over it. And y'all, where were we laying at that very moment? Yes, a *green pasture*! God gave me peace and quietness, and He restored my soul. His rod and His staff were my comfort. He sternly, with His rod, delivered me from evil and then led me with His staff to the pasture of peace. Goodness and love followed me that day and every day since. And guess what, my cup overflows, and I will dwell in the house of the Lord forever! It turned out that even if I wanted to doubt that God had truly prepared Tyler for my healing, I couldn't have because two days prior, he already knew the scripture to quote for how that day would happen. He kept quiet about it because I wouldn't have believed him if he had told me.

That day, my depression ended. The spirit of depression had left and would never return because I had a promise from God. He used my husband to heal me.

Yes, His rod disciplines us, but it also fights off anything that tries to harm us.

Let's study spirits briefly. If you have the Holy Spirit living inside you, you cannot be possessed by a demonic spirit because the Holy Spirit has already taken up residence and is dwelling within you. A spirit—rather the Holy Spirit or demonic—has to be invited, in some way, to dwell within you. When you ask Jesus to be the Savior of your life and live inside of you, you invited the Holy Spirit. Although we can't be possessed, we can, however, be oppressed. But just like Jesus, we have authority over them.

Take a look at two of the many proofs of spirits in the Bible. Read Ephesians 6:12. Now read 2 Timothy 1:7.
What spirit did God not give us?

_____

God gave us the Holy Spirit, and through the Holy Spirit, He gives us many things.

What three things are mentioned in this verse?

_____

_____

_____

These three things are the opposite of fear, and they overcome fear. So we know that fear does not come from the Lord, yet it says spirit. As Christians, we still have fear sometimes, but if it is overwhelming fear, you can bet that's the enemy. I just love that we are given the power to overcome the evil spirits of fear. Surely, that can make even the driest bones rattle!

If any, what spirits plague you today? I pray your answer is none, but if I'm right, I'm betting you have at least one or you wouldn't still be reading this book. Ask God to open your heart and your mind so that you can see and hear.

_____

_____

_____

_____

_____

_____

_____

_____

_____

_____

Remember, as a Christian, you have power to defeat the enemy. You also have angels encamped around you, protecting you. The enemy cannot kill you! They are not able to control you like that, but you do have control over them.

Take comfort in God's rod and His staff!

Here's another drawing box for you.

Don't forget to pray!

CHAPTER 4

───ᴍ───

Why Fathers Say No

God called Tyler home from that old oil rig and called us into ministry.

After the day of my healing, Tyler didn't go back to the rig. We were nervous to say the least, but we knew we had a call on our lives. In faith, we borrowed money and bought a sporting goods store. With God's help, we made it flourish.

Once we got it on its feet, we took a youth pastor's position at a local church and served there for two years. We felt our work was complete there, so we began to pray about where to go next. We still had our store. It still operated well and provided us a comfortable living, but we knew that wasn't all God had for us to do. We both knew a ministry position was where God wanted us most. We just had no clue where.

I was a thirty-one-year old woman walking down an old country road with my husband. While talking about our next steps and where God would lead us to go, our Lord used a snake. Yep, God can and will use anyone and anything to do a work for Him. I don't know about you, but there are two creatures I hate most in life, and one of those is a snake. Any size, any kind, any color—I hate them all. The other is a roach, but that's beside the point.

On our morning walk that day, God allowed my scariest enemy to be stretched across almost the entire road. Again, it was a small country road that barely fits two cars, and I don't remember what kind of snake it was, but nonetheless, I had a very unhealthy fear of it. I feel sure I turned the other direction and probably wanted to run.

How many times do we do that exact same thing when it comes to the enemy? My husband calmed me and taught me to be still and wait for it to pass, just the same as God does for us. Then God gave Tyler a word for us both. It was kind of the same thing as an object lesson in children's church but not quite as simple and far scarier. This was a powerful word from the Lord. The snake represented what was about to come in our near future. There would be a snake (serpent) in our path, blocking the way. If we cowered down to it, then it would continue to stand in our way and slither its way right into our lives.

This is what it looked like. Haha.

Always write down what God shows and/or says to you. You will need to see it again at some point in your life!

You're about to get a quick, diluted version of a year's span, so read carefully and fill in the blanks of your mind.

The days went on and we continued to pray, forgetting all about God's warning to us. We both forgot about the snake in the road, which was Satan's plan all along, and our store that we worked so hard to build began to take a turn for the worse under circumstances that seemed so completely out of my control. Reasons that were so far from my fault, but were in the hands of my precious husband. He had made a huge mistake. He ordered thousands of dollars over budget in inventory without consulting me, the office manager.

DO YOU SEE THAT SNAKE IN THE ROAD?

In the meantime, we got another opportunity to serve in the church. This time, it was in children's ministry, and I was pumped. As I got it off its feet and going well, I began to notice more and more, each week that went by, I was doing this all alone. No matter how many times I asked, Tyler just wasn't helping with the load at all.

THERE'S THAT SNAKE AGAIN!

My beloved, the one that had so irresponsibly sunk our business, slowly became the husband that wouldn't pray with me and wouldn't help me with anything. He turned into the man that took a check with his name on it from the church each month that I earned, as if he was taking credit for it. He was the husband that worked so many hours that we rarely saw him, yet we still struggled financially. How could that be? He was no longer my hero; and just as much as a man needs to be a hero, a woman wants her husband to be her hero.

ANOTHER SNAKE IN THE ROAD!

To make ends meet, I began renovating homes and restoring furniture. I heard God tell me so clearly not to do it. He told me to do only ministry work, to work for the Lord and focus daily on it, but I just couldn't see why I should let my family suffer and do without what we were accustomed to having. So I disobeyed. The busier my business became, the less time I had for God and for the children's ministry He had given us, but I pushed through each day and made it work.

SNAKE!

Most days, as I worked tirelessly on ministry, homes, and furniture, my own housework, raising two sons, and helping them with extreme amounts of homework, I would ask myself why this man of mine just refused to be who God called him to be. I thought deeply on why he put me in the position to have to pay so hard for his mistakes and irresponsible choices, day in and day out, while still having dinner on the table each night when he got home. I felt like a slave and most days like a single mother. I was not being taken care of emotionally, physically, or spiritually by the man that used to be my dream come true.

Still, I prayed for myself, my husband, and our marriage until the day someone knocked on the door and handed me papers. We had been served. The company that Tyler had ordered too much inventory from was suing us. And guess what they were allowed to take? *Our home.*

SNAKE!

We had done everything possible to pay what we owed, but my perfect credit score was about to be snatched away, along with trust and respect for the man I had built my whole life around. Suddenly, all of the things that he had done to me and all of the things that he had said to me in the past began to affect me in a way that they never had before.

I began to focus deeply on how he left me when we had only been married four and a half years and how he took every red cent we had, leaving me with two tiny babies and no money, all because he decided he wanted to live a different kind of life. He decided drinking, partying, and strip clubs would take the place of his marriage.

The worst part was he let me blame myself for ruining our marriage. He resented me because I had to lead our home since he wouldn't step up to the plate. In the two months that Tyler was gone, he told me countless times that nothing we owned was mine. He was the only one who worked outside of the home, paid for it all, and my name was on nothing. Though I had forgiven him with open arms between those years, I made sure I worked and bought things in my name to build my credit. Now he was having it taken away from me, just like he had told me all those years ago, and I had no choice but to watch it all go away.

I remembered all the times he would purposely lie straight to my face over and over again about all things big and small, whether they mattered or not. I started noticing how he didn't take time to make sure he did the things most important to me and how he never noticed when manly duties needed to be taken care of. I noticed how he couldn't seem to remember a single thing that mattered and how he didn't listen to a word I said.

SNAKE!

Yes, it was that bad! But why had I never noticed any of this before? Had I been blind all of this time?

It was because I had stopped being the praying wife I had always been because I was tired of praying for us and doing all of the work while he never seemed to meet me in the middle.

SNAKE!

Remember my struggle with being perfect that I told you about at the beginning of the book? After giving it every bit of energy we had, the day had come. We had to file for bankruptcy. The woman who had perfect everything and worked her butt off to make sure everything stayed that way had the shame of losing it all, even my very own mind.

SNAKE!

We found a lawyer and got started. He assured me, since I went alone, that we had nothing to worry about. He let me know he would take very good care of us, along with several flirty words. After a few too many unnecessary phone calls, he finally had my trust. I felt taken care of.

Needless to say, the enemy was opening my eyes and swinging doors open to very bad territory, places I had never even thought of going before. He blinded my eyes to all things good and opened them to all things that seemed good but were actually meant to destroy me. He opened my eyes to a wolf in sheep's clothing—Satan in an expensive suit. Don't act like you don't know what I mean. It can happen, ladies.

For the next few weeks, that same wolf told me all the things a woman wants to hear, and he pushed until I found myself in the middle of a full-blown phone affair. I pushed God and my husband out of my mind and welcomed that snake I had feared so much to slither right into my life, just like God had shown us.

I very quickly recognized Satan's plan for me, so I dodged the next flaming arrow Satan had pointed directly at me. I wouldn't agree to see the lawyer in person, and it ended. I so remorsefully told Tyler everything that had happened. I repented and received forgiveness from God and my hubby. I stepped down from teaching children's church because we felt that was the right thing to do for a time, and Tyler took over. *Finally*, he *had* to help! Although I had not prayed them in a long time, this was an answer to my prayers, or so I thought.

CHAPTER 5

From One Flesh to Four

I was a thirty-two-year-old woman when spiritual warfare began *again*! And the length of time it lasted will blow your mind. I didn't choose it, I didn't want it, and I didn't invite it, but I allowed it because I didn't *run hard* toward God the way I should have.

I was still bitter and still not feeling the desire to pray. I never thought it could be possible to just feel nothing, but I was there. And even when I wanted to feel, I just couldn't. I couldn't feel the deep love for my Savior as I once had. The blinders that I had allowed Satan to slowly cover my eyes with were far too dark to see even a peek of light. Part of me wanted God, but for the first time in fourteen years, I didn't know how I would ever fully return to Him.

I still resented all that my husband had done to me. I felt shame for what I had done to him, but not a godly shame; it was a prideful shame. I wanted no one to know. Although I didn't realize it at the time, true sorrow for what I had done to him somehow got lost in the justification for all he had done to me.

For the next ten months, I grew more and more disgusted and bitter toward the man I married. I watched him teach a group of children that deserved to be taught the word of God by a man far better than the one who had barely prepared for the service and seemed to wing it most of the time. So each week I would clean up what I thought was the mess he made by going over each thing he said to make sure the children understood.

I knew I couldn't teach them again because my heart and soul were not in the right place, so I had to let him continue. I couldn't bear to watch the way it was being done anymore, so I skipped the services a lot. I needed to go into an adult service, but my pride was too big for that. I would disappoint others if I did such a shameful thing. So I stayed home most of the time. Somewhere along the way, I watched my husband, the children's ministry pastor, start drinking on Saturday and then go wing another service on Sunday. At this point, I couldn't stand it anymore, so I asked him to resign. I knew neither of us were fit for this position that God had once entrusted us with.

It seems so clear now for me as the writer and you as the reader to see exactly how plain this is and how the enemy had us both where he wanted us, but at the time, it was not so clear. Satan made it seem all so jumbled up and messy to the point that Tyler was able to justify his behavior, and because of his duty as a man to provide for his family, the money made him stay. I'm sure by now you know the pattern enough to see that my disgust with his behavior was now even deeper. Now, it had become with him as a person.

HERE'S THE SNAKE AGAIN!

Tyler began to turn his lying into an even better art. He now knew how to not only lie but successfully twist each and every conversation into *his* lies and wrongs being my fault. Still to this day, I cannot and do not want to understand how he did it because nobody can win against a person like me. I have the memory of an elephant and the skills of a CSI agent, but somehow he got better and better at his new talent. I felt defeated. There was no returning from this. Our marriage felt like a prison. All we did was argue, so Satan sent another, yes, *another* man.

No sooner than I turned this man down, I discovered that four thousand dollars was missing from the money I had saved up. The man that once told me what was his, and his *only*, now argued that he thought he could take what he wanted because it was *ours*, and without discussion at that. Not only did he take the money behind my back, he also rewrote the paper that I had in the safe with it to trick me into believing I never had that money to begin with. That man I turned down soon became an affair on and off for the next, well, let's just say a long time. I needed someone to rescue me, and Satan heard my plea.

SNAKE!

Tyler started working out at a gym for the first time in our married life. The more he worked out, the buffer he became. The more buff he became, the angrier and meaner he got toward me. I became afraid of him. He had roid rage. My Tyler became someone else. He was taking any and what seemed like everything he could get his hands on to get bigger and stronger. Then suddenly, neither of us were faithful to the other. Tyler left me *again*! We had both broken the vows that we meant so much on a beautiful evening in March of 2003.

AT LEAST FOUR SNAKES GO HERE!

This time, when the man I barely knew left me, it was just as much my fault as his. Although, neither of us knew for sure that the other had been unfaithful, it soon came to light. How? I have a praying mother, and God uses her!

As crazy as it seems, I wanted my family to stay together, so I begged God to put my marriage back together, and He did. All my prayers were answered even though I didn't understand why God would even listen to them at this point. Tyler stopped working out at the gym and taking the medicines that were giving him roid rage, and just like I had asked for, he came home. I didn't ask for a blessed or strengthened marriage; I only asked for my husband to come home.

If you think our lives were too big of a mess to even want to read it, then you should have been in it to see all the details you're not getting. Our lives were nothing short of a soap opera or a Lifetime movie. Probably, even worse! But guess what, it's not even over yet. The crazy, psycho, demonic adventure continues for another chapter.

Hang in there though because God *always wins*!

Write Luke 15:4 below.

_____

_____

_____

_____

_____

This scripture applies to you too! If you're the lost sheep today, just know that right now in this very moment, God is calling your name. Hear it getting louder? That's because the closer you get to something, the louder you hear it.

Read John 10:27–28 (NIV). Fill in the blanks below.
"My_____ _____ _____ _____ _____, I _____ them, and they _____ me. I give them eternal life, and they shall never perish; _____ _____ _____ _____ _____ _____ _____ _____ _____."

If you are saved, you are one of His sheep. That's why you hear His voice calling you. He knows us!

To know someone, you must spend time with them. His sheep truly spend time with Him, or He wouldn't know us, right? This is why on judgment day, God will say to some, "Depart from me, I never *knew* you."

God freely gives His sheep eternal life, starting the day you give your old life to Him. No one can take us away from Him, so when we get lost, He will do whatever it takes so that we may be found.

Y'all, that is *love*!

Take a minute to journal by writing how you're feeling right now. Writing out your feelings helps. God wants to hear our deepest thoughts. It helps us in our praying.

_____
_____
_____
_____
_____
_____
_____
_____
_____
_____
_____
_____
_____
_____
_____
_____
_____

Here is your drawing box

Now put on your armor and get ready for battle because the war isn't over yet.

CHAPTER 6

Suit Up

I was a thirty-four-year-old woman. A little more than a month had gone by. Already, the honeymoon phase had ended. We had to find a new home church because like any pastor would, ours asked us to step down. We struggled to find a church that was a good fit for us not only because we were Pentecostal and lived in a small town, which meant there were few churches, but because we needed it to meet the needs of a man, woman, and two teen boys.

The struggle was real. The longer it took, the easier it was to give up. It was a frustrating process, especially since we weren't doing any studying or praying on our own. We wanted a church to basically make us want to chase after God. We just couldn't get to that point again even after all those years of serving God faithfully.

The truth is, I am not myself without God leading me, so making a decision as big as a church to call home wasn't a decision I could make without Him. And neither could Tyler. So we just didn't, and guess what? Satan quickly stepped right back in. We weren't feeding the spirit, so we were feeding our flesh. That heroic husband that I so desperately wanted and dreamed of getting back never showed up. In fact, he became just the opposite.

Tyler went back into the oil field, leaving for two weeks out of each month and giving us both too much freedom and time to think. We started a competition of whose wrongdoings were worse. Every time I felt like we were making progress, the blame game started again.

I knew I wanted our marriage back, but it takes two and I just couldn't seem to get it there on my own. I needed God, but I wouldn't ask Him. I tried to do it alone. I became beatdown with shame and guilt until I felt like I had no more fight in me. Our children were tired. I was tired. Tyler was tired. But the fighting continued anyway. Here's a simplified version of the process to help you see it without a long, drawn-out chapter of reading more demonic nonsense.

Trying to giving up to trying to giving up to messing up big.

It was a vicious cycle over and over again. I wanted us but not *this* us!

Trying to work through a shattered marriage without God in the middle, without that third strand in the cord, looked something like this.

This is ours; but I can bet they are all about the same: resentment and fear; guilt and shame; looking for fixes; needing happiness and finding it elsewhere; no trust at all; more fighting; locked and/or hidden phones; *lies, lies, and more lies*; no longer talking at all because it just turned into arguing; no date nights; no family time.

But then, a light appeared. We visited our old church—our very first church, the one I had gone to for years and years before I even knew Tyler. We visited the church we thought we'd never return to, and Tyler felt a strong pull to make that our home again. How he felt that way, I didn't know because he wasn't even praying. God is just that amazing. I was so excited and finally hopeful for our future. I decided and was truly determined to go after God again. While finding new love with my Savior, I fell in love with Tyler again. But y'all, it still only got worse.

I could feel it, I could see it, I could read it as clear as an open book—the same thing that had happened before was happening again. The roid rage was back. The empty looks were there. His interest in returning to the old us was completely gone. His truck stayed locked, and the keys were always hidden again. His need to blame me for the failure of everything was so strong. He made me fear him even more than ever before. He didn't call me at all or respond to my texts unless it was about our boys. He wouldn't tell me he loved me very often. He acted crazy at both sons' ball games. He was drinking and doing things he didn't normally do behind my back. He was cursing and hiding his phone. No matter how much I cried or how hard I begged and argued, he wouldn't stop, and he wouldn't admit anything.

Don't forget about the snake!

Then it happened. It was the shock of my life! Only one year and eight months after we had put our family back in the same home, over the phone, while on the rig, Tyler told me it was over. He wanted a divorce! It was different this time; I knew he meant it. He had never said those exact words before. He had said he was unsure in the past, but he had never said the word *divorce.*

I feel sure you're rolling your eyes by now. Listen, never underestimate the power of the enemy. He is strong, and he always has a plan for our lives. The good news is God has a plan too!

CHAPTER 7

―⚬―

From a Staff to a Snake

God is near to the brokenhearted. I am a thirty-seven-year-old woman begging God once again for my marriage. No matter how much I begged, it was obvious Tyler wasn't coming back to me or God. This time, it was far more hurtful than the other two times. Why? Because God had had enough of Satan's junk. The spiritual war was about to be won for good. Like pottery, just before it's finished and beautiful, we go through fire. Just before the battle is over, that's when we're easiest to break.

Before you decide our heavenly Father isn't as good as people say He is, let's take a minute to look up two scriptures.

As always, please write them.
James 1:2–4

_____

_____

_____

_____

_____

_____

_____

_____

God is a good father because He allows us to go through trials of many kinds. He allows this because of the person it makes us become.

He loves us far too much to let us live lives that aren't the *best* for us. He doesn't just want us to make it to heaven and that's all. Do you want your child to just *make it* through school, in their marriage, or in their job? No. I bet you want them to be their best no matter how hard it is at the time because you know what being their best will bring to their future.

1 Corinthians 10:21

_____

_____

_____

God is jealous *for* us. We are the same way with our children. Sharing them with someone we know for sure is only out to kill them would bring war. Don't you think? God loves us even more than a mother loves her children. He fights for us so that we won't die to Satan's schemes for or souls. Look at the last sentence in verse 22.

Are we stronger than He? Can our blinded will that comes from the enemy possibly be stronger than God?

In verse 21, it clearly says that we *cannot* serve both God and Satan, so if you're a child of God, *he will win the war* in the end even if at first it's against our will.

WE ARE NOT STRONGER THAN GOD!

Tyler got home from the rig just a few days after telling me he wanted a divorce. I hoped to see a man I recognized when he arrived, but instead I saw a man I had never seen before. The other two times he left me, there was at least sympathy and remorse on his face and in his voice. But this time, there was no question he was done. Hatred was his most obvious feeling toward me.

The very first thing he said was, "Sit down and let's go over who gets what in the divorce." As I started begging for him to change his mind, he was pointing out furniture he wanted. His eyes were cold and blank. His attitude was that of a man I had only seen in movies—the kind of movies where the wife was mentally abused so badly that she ended up in an institute because her husband stole the kids and ran away with them and their new young stepmom, never to be seen again. Oh, how that hurt! I can almost feel it all over again as I sit here and write.

Tyler was supposed to pick up our two boys from school that afternoon as he always did when he was home from work, but the closer it got to three o'clock and seeing how he didn't show up, the more I began to panic. I called him, only to hear the voice of an almost drunk man tell me he was on the way. Who was this monster?

I fell to my knees and cried out to God because I knew I had officially lost my love forever this time. As much as it hurt, I couldn't let him pick our boys up from school. This could not be Tyler Patrick McCraw I was dealing with anymore. This was Satan himself.

Those blinders that Satan loves so much had not only been put back on my husband's eyes but on his heart as well. It had been completely hardened. I could see it so clearly, but I couldn't do a thing about it. I just had to watch it happen. His personality had completely changed. If I didn't know better, I would have sworn this was Tyler's evil twin that came to earth and swapped places with him.

As the war waged on spiritually and in our home, the evidence of the enemy taking over Tyler and our home became more and more obvious.

Let's take a look at the word *sorcery*. The Greek word is *pharmakia*. Ring a bell? *Pharm*—pharmaceutical; pharmacy. Now let's look at one of the definitions for *pharmacy*, paying close attention to the first two words.

Pharmacy—the *art*, practice, or profession of preparing, preserving, compounding, and dispensing medical drugs.

Read Exodus 7:1–13 and come right back. Look closely at the end of verse 11. It says they did the same things by their secret *arts*. Guess what a sorcerer's secret *art* is? Potions (drugs or medicines).

Just like they turned the staff into a snake, they turned people into someone completely opposite of who they were. Look how opposite a staff is from a snake. A staff is used by a shepherd to *care* for sheep. By leading and guiding them with it, he keeps them safe. A snake *cares* about no one but itself.

Do you think for one second that Satan doesn't use the same the schemes and tricks he always has? Why would he fix what isn't broken? It still works y'all!

That's exactly what he used to completely change my husband—drugs (medicines).

By the way, I'm not against the good works that drugs (medicines) do for people, but they can certainly be used by the enemy to do harm. In fact, all things intended for good can be used to harm. No, I am not saying your pharmacist is a sorcerer. Haha!

The Bible tells us in the book of Romans that God works all things for the good of those who love Him, who have been called according to His purpose.

While the suffering and the heartache continued and the agony of watching the father of my children become—well, I'll just say it—an evil stranger, I still was not letting go of our marriage. I slowly began to hear the voice of the Lord telling me not to give up. My world was falling apart all around me, but keep reading and watch the journey begin while the drama continued.

Look up Psalm 34:17 and write it below.

_____

_____

_____

_____

Who are the righteous? Romans 3:22

_____

_____

_____

By faith alone, we are made righteous. So yes, I was righteous even after all I had done. I had sincerely asked for it and had been forgiven. Now read Psalm 34:18 and write it below.

_____

_____

_____

Why do you think God is near to the brokenhearted?

_____

_____

_____

Let's look it up: James 4:8 (NIV).
_____ near to _____ and he will _____.

We draw near to Him when our hearts are broken. He is always there, waiting for us to come near to Him.

If you're a parent and you know your child is heartbroken, you want to hold them and help them through it, but they have to allow you to do so. Just the same yet even more, God sees every tear we cry, and He wants to hold us and help us through it.

Have you ever thought about all of the scriptures that say God will help us *through* it? It says *through* it because it does not mean He will take it away. There is no lesson that can be learned if He fixes it *for* us! Right?

Read Isaiah 43:2 and highlight the word *through* in your Bible.

Here's one last verse I want you to look up for me—Psalm 147:3.

What does it say He does to the brokenhearted?

_____

What does it say He does to their wounds?

_____

Look up and write the definitions of the following.

*Heal*_____

*Bind*_____

*Cohere*_____

He loves us so much that He makes our wounds whole again!

Are there wounds that you need our heavenly Father to make whole again?

Don't put a Band-Aid over it again today. Ask God to help you trust Him enough to give those wounds over to Him.

Write it down and pray circles around it.

_____

_____

_____

_____

Perhaps, God heals our hearts but binds up our wounds because wounds are just a little slower to heal. It's through our healed hearts that our wounds become healed. Wow!

Chapter 8

The Journey

I fought, and I mean I fought, *hard*! I had to sit back and watch Tyler change our joint Facebook account into two separate accounts. He changed *my* profile picture and information then set up a new private one for himself. Now the world knew. We were officially known as separated!

I fought, but I fought wrong until the journey began. Some people had noticed the change in Tyler's attitude, personality, behavior, and the look in his eyes. They heard him yell. They watched him drive like a teenaged boy that just got his first truck with loud pipes and would go zero to sixty in five seconds flat.

They saw him leave us and go out doing only God knows what during a tornado that hit our home while ignoring our calls for help. They saw him wreck his truck and then, a few days later, wreck our son's first truck. Police witnessed things he did and got phone calls from people all around, filing complaints about him. We even had cops ride by our home every so often, making sure everything was okay. People saw a lot, but what they didn't see was far more painful than what they did.

They didn't see him break down doors or threaten me in ways that were terrifying on multiple occasions. They didn't see him try to take everything from us. They didn't see him tell our two sons to lie to me. They couldn't see the damage his behavior was causing our sons, or the birthday party children were unable to come to because of fear *that Daddy* could possibly be there. Nor did they see the brokenness it caused when he wouldn't attend.

They couldn't possibly see the broken hearts of two boys and a mom/wife when his appearance became less and less. And there was no way they could ever see the hurt and fear it caused when this strange man began breaking into the house while we were sleeping, or the agony of him making up stories to tell family and friends so that he appeared a little more innocent in his wrongdoing.

Even more than the battles and fights that went on behind closed doors, the boys that were being torn apart, and the brokenness of a wife and mother, people were unable to see what God was doing in me. And they weren't able to see His plan and how it would all work for good. Even when we don't see it, God is working! On February 19, 2020, my journey began. My pastor, C. A. Farmer, taught on spiritual disobedience, and God opened my eyes that very night.

> *I can't fix the ministry I left, but I can begin this new one.
>
> *Focus on others (Aunt Cindy)
> -Open my eyes to the harvest
> -Fix my disobedience by asking forgiveness and ministering in another way (stop my business)
> -Use what I'm going through to help others
> -Get one of my five in the process
> *Do it anyway, no matter what
> NO MATTER HOW I FEEL, DO IT ANYWAY!
>
> *Judgment will be easier on those who never knew than those who know but do not do it.
> *That's disobedience.*
> Disobedience is SO, SO, SO BAD!

*Luke 1:17
DEMONS SUBMIT to us in Jesus's name.
*Luke 1:18—WOW
We must be pleasing to the father

*Talk to my boys about choosing a spouse, by how her family is, as well as how she is. Talk about a family with blessings and a separate family with curses. A family of addicts and a family of God!

I disobeyed God the summer of 2016, I'm going to clean up my mess NOW, February 2020!

*I can't fix the ministry I left
but I can begin this new one)

* Focus on others) (Aunt Cindy)
- open my eyes to the Harvest
- fix my disobedience by asking
- forgiveness & ministering in
- another way (STOP MY BUSINESS)
- use what I'm going through
- to help others)
- Get 1 of my 5 in the process
* DO IT ANYWAY - no matter what
NO MATTER HOW I FEEL - DO IT
ANYWAY!!!

*Judgement will be easier on those
who never knew, that those who
know but do not do it *That's
(disobedience *
Disobedience is so so so BAD!!!
* Luke 1:17
DEMONS SUBMIT to us in Jesus'
NAME
* Luke 1:18 - WOW
- we must be pleasing to the Father

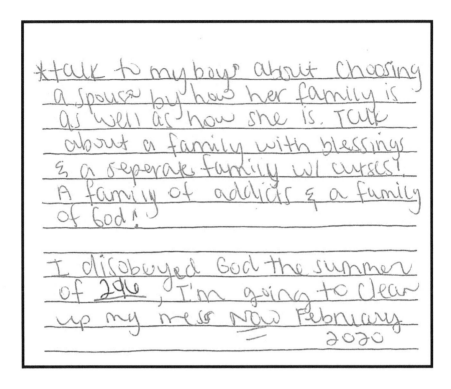

talk to my boys about choosing a spouse by how her family is as well as how she is. Talk about a family with blessings & a seperate family w/ curses. A family of addicts & a family of God!

I disobeyed God the summer of 246, I'm going to clean up my mess NOW February 2020

It was that night that I allowed the Lord to begin a new work in me. I slowly began to let go and let God. I still fought wrongly at times. I still had a shattered heart. I still screamed and cried and even felt like dying at times. I was still so angry with Tyler, but this was the beginning.

On February 25, just two days after receiving a message from God in tongues from Troy Dew, and interpreted by our pastor—to think on the things that bring joy and not dwell on the things that drag me to the ground—I started walking at the track.

Little did I know, each night as I walked, I would hear from our heavenly Father. When I tell you God saw me and carried me all the way *through* this, I mean He was *never,* not on time. In the exact moments I fell apart, He would send help. He even sent four of my dearest friends, one at a time, to the track one night when I thought I couldn't make it any longer. I can't wait to tell you all about more of those times, but for now, let's go to February 25.

Let's go back to the track on the first night.

As I walked with earbuds in my ears, listening to "Raise a Hallelujah" on repeat, the Lord began to speak to me about pride. He told me to stop worrying about the opinion of others and focus on Him and Him only. Before I tell you the rest, let me remind you that I was at a public track, but y'all, God don't care. He straight up does not care where you are. If it's for your good or to fulfill His plan, He will *ask* you to do embarrassing things. Will He make you? No, absolutely not, but He sure will ask you. And considering the outcome, I recommend you obey.

Here's the conversation between God and myself after He spoke to me about pride.

> GOD. SING IT.
> ME. BUT, GOD, people are out here. And Lord, I have earbuds in my ears. That makes you sound terrible and that's just embarrassing.
> GOD. SING IT.
> ME. I raise a hallelujah, in the presence of my enemies (singing as I walk a full lap and my breath begins to shorten).

GOD. SING LOUDER.

ME. BUT, GOD, (as I sang louder) I'm gonna sing in the middle of the storm, louder and louder, you're gonna hear my praises roar

GOD. LOUDER.

ME. (As I finished my second lap and sounded worse) Up from the ashes, hope will arise. Death is defeated, the king is alive.

GOD. Keep singing! I know you want to raise your hands. Go ahead and do that now. Victory comes through praise.

ME. SING A LITTLE LOUDER (with my hands raised) IN THE PRESENCE OF MY ENEMIES. SING A LITTLE LOUDER, LOUDER THAN THE UNBELIEF. SING A LITTLE LOUDER, MY WEAPON IS A MELODY. SING A LITTLE LOUDER, HEAVEN COMES TO FIGHT FOR ME!

REPEAT.

LOUDER AND LOUDER, YOU'RE GONNA HEAR MY PRAISES ROAR

REPEAT THE SONG.

This continued for about ten more laps, I guess, and by the end of the song, I was on that track with my hands raised all the way to heaven, singing as loudly as I could. I never cared that a cop drove by, the church next door that had the door open while they worked closed it because of me, and the lights had flipped on in a house next to the track. I had been made new, and that's all that mattered to me! I had finally dropped my pride, and I was able to focus only on myself and God. My lessons from that experience were many.

I was able to call on people for prayer and ask for help. I needed them, but God couldn't use them if I kept to myself because of worry of what they would think. My mistakes from the past no longer held me hostage. I was no longer afraid of being blamed for the condition of my marriage by others due to my silence and Tyler's loudness on the matter. I no longer let my mistakes define me. I was able to talk about my past with no fear of being judged. I began to see myself in a different light.

What that experience did for me later was and is even better than what it did at that point.

Naturally, Tyler and I had left the boys out of the loop on mistakes made in our marriage. But after that night, though I didn't truly know why, I felt that I should tell them all about the mistakes I had made. So I did. They could clearly see what their daddy was doing, so I didn't have to tell them about his mistakes, or my own for that matter. But I couldn't stop myself from telling them.

I constantly made sure they knew this wasn't their daddy. It was the enemy we were fighting against so that couldn't have been my only reason for telling on myself. I never quite put my finger on it back then, but now I know why. They *had* to know because they will hear our testimony and read this book someday. Do you see it? God goes before us and takes care of things in advance!

I have a recording from that night. If you would like to listen to it, go to Bitty from Ashes (YouTube channel) and watch "Becoming Obedient."

These things and more happened to me during Tyler's time away at work for two weeks, but that didn't stop the drama the next time he came home. Unfortunately, the hurt became even worse, and his actions were out of control. It wasn't just him. Some of my actions became out of control as well. But God…

Can I ask you to turn on "Raise a Hallelujah" and turn it up loud? Sing it until your praise is louder than any unbelief in your life. When you're done, come back here and finish up what God has for you.

What is pride?

Write your own definition without looking it up before you continue reading.

_____

_____

_____

Pride is preferring self-will to God's will. It's pretty much saying, "I know more than you, God."

Do you have pride that is blocking you from becoming the woman or man that God knows you are?

It can range anywhere from giving your heart to God for the very first time, to marriage situations, all the way to seasoned Christians that are disobedient to God's perfect will for them, resulting in living in His permissive will.

If you answered yes, then take some time to write below. Then draw in your box.

_____

_____

_____

_____

_____

_____

_____

_____

_____

_____

_____

_____

CHAPTER 9

A Torch of Golden Nuggets

Tyler had convinced his mother, brother, grandmother, and other family members that he was doing no wrong. While they could see that something wasn't quite right, he was very convincing. He led them to believe I wouldn't let him see our boys and that all of this was my fault. Everything that happened, he twisted and made it the opposite of what it actually was.

I begged Tyler to spend time with Mason and Ty Majer, but he couldn't be convinced mainly because that would blow his story to his family but also because he thought he had better things to do. I had to pull myself together to help our children make it through such a hard time. It almost seemed impossible to do at times. I would take them fishing with a lump in my throat. I made birthday cakes with anger in my heart. I cooked dinner with panic of the future on my mind. I would do Bible studies, go to church, and teach/learn manly duties with my boys with fear in my spirit. And I would take the boys on little getaway trips with anxiety in my chest and trembling in my voice.

The boys and I left for the beach with some friends, leaving Tyler for the very first spring break trip ever, and to top it off, it was on our wedding anniversary. I felt such a sickness in my stomach the moment my tires hit the road. I felt like crying the entire way to what should have been a fun trip. I saw the hurt all over Ty Majer, and I felt the hurt all inside of me. I can confidently say it was the worst decision I could've made. You simply cannot force fun when you're going through pain that is most comparable to the pain that Jesus endured on the cross. Why is it comparable? Because I was paying for the sins of another while my heart was filled with love, yet shattered into pieces. I felt rejected, broken, and deeply wounded.

As I took out my wallet to pay for dinner on night two of our trip, I checked our bank account online to see if I should pay with cash or card, and I don't know if I'll ever forget the way my heart sank right there in front of hundreds of people. I saw a payment to a club/ restaurant that was far too large to have been for one person.

I knew Tyler had changed. I knew he was drinking. I knew he didn't want the lifestyle of being the family man he once was, but this was over the top! A club? Paying for someone else? I immediately wanted to fight God about the whole *holding-on* thing.

There just seemed to be no way to hold on any longer. I ran to the closet the moment we got back to the condo so the boys wouldn't hear me crying for help from God. I couldn't let them hear me beg Him to hold me and comfort me. I needed my father to send *help*! And once again, He did.

That night as I rested peacefully, I had a wonderful dream. God comforted me in a different way than expected. He let me see my brother and hear his voice, just as you can hear and see the person next to you for the first time in over twenty years. And guess what? Justie held me!

He saw me crying and invited me to lay my head on his chest, then he wrapped his arms around me. I was so blessed because I didn't just wake up and Justie was gone; he let me know he had to go. As I watched him go away, I saw him with a torch made of golden nuggets in his hand. He handed this torch to a girl, then I woke up.

Once we were home, I told my mom all about the dream and how wonderful it was. I tried to describe the way the torch looked but with no luck, so I decided to Google it in hopes of showing her. I didn't really know what the torch part of the dream meant, but that didn't last long. I never found the image I was looking for on the internet, but what I found will forever be just as wonderful as the way I felt lying in my brother's arms.

It was the explanation of the torch made of golden nuggets. I wasn't looking for it and I didn't even know I cared about what it meant. I was just so happy about being with my brother again for that small amount of time and for the comfort God sent to me, even if it was only in a dream. But God knew I needed to know the meaning. To save a lot of time and reading, I'll give you the short version.

Read Job 22:21–30 and write what verse 24 says about the torch I saw in my dream below.

_____

_____

_____

The NIV translation says, "And assign your nuggets to the dust, your gold of Ophir to the rocks in the ravines." Ophir is a port or region mentioned in the Bible famous for its wealth. King Solomon received cargo from Ophir every three years. It consisted of gold, silver, sandalwood, pearls, ivory, apes, and peacocks (1 Kings 10:22).

This was the second part of my journey—the missing puzzle piece, I guess you could say—that would reveal it all. It was confirmation to me in the best form that God had already sent to me from a dear friend from my church. Just a few months before, God had her tell me to clean my vessel and get rid of all the filth and idols that were clouding my spiritual vision and causing warfare. (Sidenote, He had her tell Tyler the same thing.)

I needed to turn those nuggets of gold into dust and trust God. The fear of my future had to be turned into peace, and the things that were bringing me no good had to go down with my unbelief. March 18, 2020, just nine days after the dream, God told me to burn some of my most-prized possessions, and I knew why those possessions had to go.

So at 10:04 p.m., I started a fire. Now listen to the best part that I didn't think of until the fire had burned down and the hot ashes went cold. The next morning, I walked out into my backyard to look once more at the place where I had thrown my second set of golden nuggets and lit those jokers up, like it was the Fourth of July.

I had to see the place again where freedom rang the night before and the spot where I had rejoiced and praised God because I was free from my second set of chains. First, pride, then possessions that held me to an ungodly lust. I can still feel how excited I was that morning as I walked toward the dust of my past mistakes, blowing in the wind.

I felt a complete halt spiritually and physically. I feel sure I stopped walking for a moment because it hit me like a ton of bricks, *dust*! A light bulb came on in my mind. That was why God had me burn it, not simply throw it away.

He wanted it to be symbolic just like His word says in Job. He wanted me to be able to see my gold turn to dust, not only in my spirit but with my eyes. I could see it clearly without one bit of cloudiness in my vision. My vessel was being cleansed, and my nuggets were turning to dust.

The stimulus and tax return money that caused the next bout of drama was not mine to store up. Even though I felt with all of my human mind I should get at least half of it, God said no. He said no because that would have only added to my nuggets. Watch how that mess turns into a message in chapter 10.

My Nuggets of Gold.

1. Pride
2. Impure possessions
3. Money

What are your nuggets of gold? Do you have idols, things that are clogging your vessel, or clouding in your spiritual vision? It certainly doesn't have to be money or possessions. It can be just about anything.

_____

_____

_____

_____

_____

Please read 2 Timothy 2:20–21. What does it say about a vessel for honor or instrument for noble purposes?

_____

_____

_____

_____

See how it makes sense now? When I was told that God said to clean my vessel, I didn't fully get it, but then it was revealed. We need to know the word of God so that we're fully able to understand when we're in times of need and when He speaks to us.

Please take time to study the Bible. Always pray before and after you read it. Be sure to be a vessel of honor. Cleanse yourself with things from God. If your vision is cloudy or your vessel is clogged with filth and unrighteousness, not fit to honor God, then Satan has a very big foothold in your life.

Ask God to help you clean it up today and then be sure to keep it as clean as you want your house when new company is coming over.

Go back and read all of 2 Timothy 2 just because it's so good. Here's your drawing box

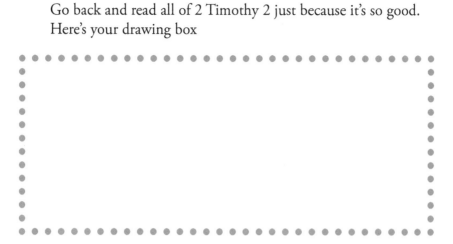

As always, draw something that helps you remember what you learned today and something that represents what you wrote about.

CHAPTER 10

Message from a Mess

Next, I watched Tyler take all the stimulus money from COVID-19 and the income tax money, and move it all from our joint checking account into a new one he opened in only his name. At first, I rushed to the bank to get a fair amount out, but at the same time, God said *no* through many scriptures. He told me to trust Him. Because I was faithfully studying His word and listening to His voice, I knew exactly the right thing to do. So yes, I watched it disappear.

I no longer had to be afraid in our own home because Tyler didn't come to our house at all anymore. The police no longer had to get involved, and I no longer had to console two hurting teen boys over what they saw their daddy doing. Now I was consoling them because they didn't see their dad at all. Satan and all his demons had stepped it up yet another notch, but so did God and all the angels.

While the demons called for more and more help to blind my husband, even more than he was before, God called me to deeper prayer and He alerted more prayer warriors. While Tyler was making choices that involved living in the home of another woman and our boys never wanting to speak to him again because he had shunned them and took on an entire new family lifestyle, God was preparing me for when the battle was finished.

Before I go into detail of my prep, let me make sure you read that correctly. My husband's body was staying at the home of another woman. His arms were around her and her children at bedtime. His mouth was telling them good night. His laughter was filling their rooms. His truck was parked outside of her home and his stomach was getting full at her table. But his mind, heart, eyes, and spirit were nowhere to be found. Satan had taken them away from him, but God was restoring mine.

He restored my hope and faith because my knees stayed on the floor more than my feet, my eyes on His word more than looking for evidence of Tyler's wrongs, and my mind on the promises of God more than the lies of Satan. Now I was fully able to see, and while the enemy was still able to trip me up a little sometimes, I heard the voice of the Lord more times than I can count. And I was now able to discern the voices of the enemy and know the difference between the two.

I learned if it didn't bring peace, it was not the voice of my Father. No matter the circumstance, God's rod and staff comforts us, even if it's not what we want to hear at the time. So while the world would tell me I'd be crazy to want a man that would do the things Tyler was doing to me and our sons, I could still hear the voice of the Lord louder saying, "It's not over yet. I have the final say. The battle belongs to me. Yes, divorce happens to good people, but you're not other people. I have a plan. Just hold on. You're still his wife, submit to him. Love him anyway. Don't keep a record of wrongs. Don't take the money, trust Me. Seek My kingdom first. Feed the spirit, starve, the flesh. Focus on others and help them, I'll take care of you. Sit, in peace, and let Me have control. Lift your face, bride of Christ."

But one evening in March, I heard and saw something more promising than I had heard from God throughout the entire journey thus far. He gave me a vision, and guess where I was when I saw it? Yep, you guessed it—the track!

I was walking and talking with Jesus, and He was reminding me to keep my eyes above the hills because my help comes from the Lord, the maker of heaven and earth. As I was looking up just above the trees, mixed in with many other clouds, I saw a heart-shaped cloud and with it came a vision and the voice of the Lord.

The vision was so clear. It was Tyler and I standing on a big platform, talking to couples and encouraging marriages through our testimony.

Then I heard the Lord say, "Do not let go! I am the alpha and the omega, the beginning and the end."

I continued to hear His voice when He would say, "Write it down." Each time, I would do as He instructed by writing down my journey and the things He told me. I heard His voice when He would tell me to take a picture and/or video something. Though I didn't always understand why, I never questioned Him. I just did as He said.

I always wrote it down, took pictures, and videoed just because He said so. Little did I know at the time it would all be used in so many ways to bring glory to Him. One, to outweigh pictures, writings, and videos of the bad. Two, to be a constant reminder of His blessings on us. Three, to help build His army in ways just like this book. Guess what the very first thing was that He asked me to write down? It was the vision. Read it once more and then come back.

Here's the actual page I wrote back then. I didn't write it on the day I saw the vision. It was one week later.

April 8, 2020

Vision

I am afraid of writing this just in case my faith may fail me and this doesn't come to pass, but I'm writing it anyway because I'm going to let my words and promises be louder than my unbelief.

I see (us) me and Tyler on a platform encouraging other marriages through our testimony. I saw this vision as I was walking the track one beautiful evening in March 2020.

I just can't stop believing for my marriage. As much as I shouldn't want it, the Holy Spirit within me, will not allow me to let go.

> 4-8-20
>
> -Vision-
> I am afraid of writing this
> just in case my faith may
> fail me and this doesn't come to
> pass, but I'm writing it anyway
> b/c I'm going to let my words
> and promises be louder than
> my unbelief...
>
> I see (us) me & Tyler on a
> platform encouraging other
> marriages through our
> testimony.
> I saw this vision as I walked
> the track one beautiful
> evening in march, 2020.
>
> I just can't stop believing for
> my marriage, as much as I
> shouldn't want it, the Holy
> spirit within me, will not
> let go!

That makes three times you've read it. Guess what Tyler and I are doing today? God took my fear of speaking in public and made it a divine disability so that He would receive the glory and it would bring others to Him.

What's a divine disability? As Jimmy Evans explains, it's just what I said—it's a disability given to us so that we will not be given glory for the work of the Lord.

Read Exodus 4:10. What disability did Moses have?

If Moses had been a smooth talker, then it could have been said that he talked Pharaoh right out of the Jews, but because Moses's speech was so bad, he couldn't have possibly been given the credit. The glory for the Israelites being let go belonged only to God and can only be given to Him due to Moses's disability, therefore making it a divine disability.

That's exactly what God did with me. If I wasn't afraid of public speaking, then I could discredit God in a number of ways, but because of my fear and how evident it has been, God is able to receive all the glory and fame through my testimony. It was a divine disability, and though I still get nervous, that "much-needed" divine disability that's bringing people to God is now a divine healing that's bringing marriages and families to Him.

How about you? Do you have a known or possibly unknown divine disability? Do you have a disability at all? What is it?

I bet God is going to use you through that disability in a mighty way.

The next thing God had me to write down, He confirmed through a phone call from a dear friend. If only you could have heard the actual conversation, you would have been just as amazed as Krystal and I. After a little conversation of things like, how are you doing, how are the boys, and have you heard from Tyler, she cut to the chase.

Krystal shared with me what she had felt in her spirit to tell me. She said, "Write it down, friend!" After a lengthy conversation about our amazement that God had sent her to confirm what He had already told me (because let's be real, we'll never stop being amazed when God sends confirmation that is that clear) we hung up and I started writing exactly what He said.

To be continued.

CHAPTER 11

Get Rid of It

There were times when I wanted revenge. I wanted to be able to see the revenge, but I didn't want to get revenge myself. I wanted God to do it. Why did I even think that could or would happen? Read Psalm 109. David asked for the same thing, and God, being the loving Father He is, gave me just that. But it didn't look exactly like I thought it would. God's revenge looked a bit differently from what I could have possibly imagined at the time. But the more my relationship grew with God, the more my revenge became lined up with His.

As I said before, after the short conversation with Krystal, I hung up the phone and began writing that morning. I was still in the presence of the Holy Spirit from my time in prayer, and I picked up exactly where I had left off. I wrote every word.

> I am not innocent and that's the hardest part to face.
>
> I will not dwell on this and I will accept God's grace over this.
>
> I will do it differently from this point forward.

Get behind me Satan.

I have been a liar!

I did not love the way I should have.

I was not submissive and I did not have a quiet and pure spirit.

I didn't give my whole self, and my whole heart because of fear.

I stopped praying.

I perverted sex.

I had a phone affair and a physical affair that lasted, even though I was warned time and time again, by God.

I hid money.

I took my Tyler for granted.

I held his wrongs against him, but wanted and expected grace for mine.

I blamed him over and over again.

I didn't allow him to be himself and lead the way he chose.

I put him down a lot.

I pushed him away.

I wouldn't talk and/or text when he wanted.

I stopped taking care of him.

I stopped making him feel needed and wanted.

I made him stop posting on Facebook.

I called him names and put him down even when I knew it hurt.

I made him feel stupid and dumb.

I used him for my needs.

I ended up putting him down to others.

I have been controlling.

I repaid evil for evil.

I didn't honor him and I wasn't patient with him.

I disobeyed God, and I worked anyway.

I did not help with children's church.

And now...

I lost him—the man of my dreams!

God said for me to close my ears to the world and to keep my mouth shut... Innocently I did this all wrong too.

I have told others about him and his downfalls with no grace for why he was there.

I told some of mine, but only what was obvious.

I have still kept money a secret.

I have told our boys way too much.

I have not asked God what to do nearly as much as I have asked others.

I have remained angry with him and so hurt, leaving only him to blame.

I did not do away with his wrongs the way God told me to.

I have remained focused on all of the bad and scary, and have let myself have no peace.

I continue to fight back in the flesh and not let God take care of this battle.

I continually care about what others think of me, when I've been told time and time again not to, and that causes me to fight and to do evil!

I continue to keep a record of wrongs.

I continue to find ways to place the blame.

I do not trust God, my faith is so weak, I get angry with him for my wrongs, and I lose hope almost daily.

I get angry with others, especially my mom, when I hear things, I don't want to hear, yet I'll bring them on myself.

April 10, 2020 and April 22, 2020

Ask myself, do I love?

Am I patient? No. Yes. (I'm still waiting.)

Am I kind? Not, enough. Yes. (I put him over me.)

Do I envy? Yes. No. (I don't want what he has.)

Am I proud? Yes. No (I told all my wrongs.)

Do I dishonor? Yes. No (I cover his wrongs with mine.)

Am I easily angered? Yes. No (I blocked him, so I/we couldn't fight.)

Have I and do I keep a record of wrongs? Yes. No. (I deleted them.)

Do I delight in evil? Sometimes. No. (I don't want to hurt him.)

Do I rejoice in truth? Yes. Yes.

Do I always protect? No. Yes. (I didn't tell his wrongs.)

Do I trust? No. (I'm learning.)

Do I hope? No. Yes. (I'm still waiting.)

Do I persevere? Yes. Yes.

Please read the handwritten journal entry so that this will make more sense.

①

I am not innocent & that's the hardest part to face.

* I will not dwell on this & I will accept God's grace over this. I will do it differently from this point forward. Get behind me Satan.

- I have been a liar!!!
- I did not love the way I should have
- I was not submissive & I did not have a quiet & pure spirit
- I did not give my whole self & my whole heart b/c of fear
- I stopped praying
- I perverted sex
- I had a phone affair & a physical affair that lasted even though I was warned time & time again by God
- I hid money
- I took my Tyler for granted
- I held his wrongs against him but

②

wanted & expected grace for mine
- I blamed him over & over again
- I didn't allow him to be him &
  lead the way he chose
- I put him down A LOT
- I pushed him away
- I wouldn't talk &/or text when
  he wanted
- I stopped taking care of him
- I stopped making him feel
  needed & wanted
- I made him stop posting on FB
- I called him names & put
  him down even when I knew
  It hurt
- I made him feel stupid & dumb
- I used him for my needs
- I ended up putting him down to
  others - I have been controlling
- I repayed evil for evil
- I didn't honor him & I wasn't
  patient w/ him
- I disobeyed God & worked anyway
- I did not help w/ children's church

And now...
I lost him - the man of
my dreams!

God said for me to close my
ears to the world & to keep
my mouth shut... Innocently
I did, this all wrong too...
- I have told others about
him & his downfalls w/ no
grace for why he was there.
✓ I told some of mine but only
what was obvious
✓ - I have still kept money a
secret
✓ - I have told our boys way
too much
✓ - I have not asked God what
to do near as much as I have
asked others
✓ - I have remained angry w/ him
& so hurt leaving only him to
blame
✓ - I did not do away w/ his wrongs
the way God told me to

(4)

- I have remained focused on all of the bad & the scary & have let myself have no peace
- I continue to fight back in the flesh & not let God take care of this battle
- I continually care about what others think of me when I've been told time & time again not to & that, causes me to fight & to do evil!
- I continue to keep a record of wrongs
- I continue to find ways to place the BLAME
- I do not trust God, my faith is so weak, I get angry w/ him for my wrongs, and I lose hope almost daily
- I get angry w/ others especially my mom when I hear things I don't want to hear, yet I bring them on myself

⑤

4-10-20 & 4-22-20

Ask myself...
Do I love ???

Am I patient no   yes (I'm still waiting)
Am I kind not enough yes (I put him over me)
Do I envy yes   no (I don't want what he has)
Am I proud yes   no (I told all my wrongs)
Do I dishonor yes no (I cover his wrongs
                        with mine)

Am I easily angered yes no (I blocked him so
                            I/we couldn't fight)

Have I and do I keep a record of wrongs
       yes   no (I deleted them)
Do I delight in evil sometimes   NO
                    (I don't want to
                     hurt him)

Do I rejoice in truth yes   yes
Do I always protect no   yes (I didn't tell
                            his wrongs)

       Trust no yes (I'm learning)
       Hope no   yes (I'm still waiting)
       persevere yes   yes

I was enlightened once again that day. I finally saw—and I do mean saw because it was on paper in front of me and because light had been put where darkness was before—that the man I thought was so bad couldn't possibly be any worse than I. I had been throwing stones as though I was blameless and had no sin.

I had treated my indiscretion as justice for all the things the enemy slowly deposited into my dark view of Tyler's weaknesses. I had taken off my suit of armor and saw his weaknesses through the eyes of the enemy and took them as a reason to fight *against* our marriage, empty-handed and blindfolded, instead of fighting *for* our marriage with the belt of truth buckled around my waist and the sword in my hand. I finally realized I had been fighting as though I was on the enemy's side.

Stop here for a minute and read Ephesians 6:10–18. Then come back.

That day, I saw my own sin and stopped focusing so much on Tyler's. I was able to see that all the things I thought were so terrible was just Satan's plan to kill, steal, and destroy what God has joined together.

Go back to page 3 of my journal entry and look at the very last dash. That's what makes this nugget complete and turn to dust.

Nuggets of Gold

1.   Pride
2.   Impure possessions
3.   Money
4.   Record of wrongs

Not only did I have to see my own wrongs to let the record of his past go, but I also had to let the evidence of his present wrongs go.

As the days went on, people sent pictures and new evidence of Tyler's infidelity. I wanted to keep it just in case I needed it. I believed God that my marriage would not end, but as I said before, Satan still tripped me up and planted fear from time to time. Any and all evidence was security for the outcome of the future since Tyler made it clear he didn't want to help me financially and would leave me in need, to say the least.

God had me write what love is. He had me to paint it, and He had me recite it over and over again. Every time I came to "love keeps no record of wrongs," He would say, "Get rid of all the evidence." And every time, I would fight Him on it.

Even my oldest son Mason told me I had better do it. He said, "Mama, it's like David, not needing what the world thought he'd need to fight Goliath. You don't need what the world says you'll need when fighting in a divorce. If you disobey, you know it won't end well. Trust God, Mama." Oh, the wisdom of those words from a sixteen-year-old boy.

I prayed once more and then rebuked Satan in the name of Jesus. Please take the time to listen to what God had me record that night and then come back. It's six minutes and fourteen seconds long, but listen all the way to the end. I promise it's worth it. The authority, the Holy Spirit, within me had during those six minutes gave me power like never before. We all have that authority if we have the Holy Spirit within us. It is God given.

Please go to Bitty from Ashes (YouTube channel) and listen to "Rebuking Satan April 18, 2020.'"

Two days later, I deleted it all! All of the pictures of the pills, infidelity, and drinking, videos of Tyler acting crazy, not coming home, and many more. It was all gone! Then, my prayer was answered. I began to see the revenge God was getting. His revenge was not on Tyler; it was on the enemy.

Satan was beginning to lose this battle as godly love began to fill my heart. The nugget of keeping a record of wrongs was almost gone. I could feel the chains falling, but I had one more hard step to take before it would turn completely to dust.

Rather, it's a record of wrongs you're keeping about yourself or someone else, it's still a record of wrongs that you must do away with. As I've said before, when the Bible talks about love, it means loving yourself too.

What record of wrongs are keeping you from loving yourself and/or others?

_____

_____

_____

_____

_____

_____

_____

_____

_____

As I write this, I feel the Holy Spirit telling you what to do right now. So I will stop this chapter here and give you time to listen.

When you're done listening, if you feel God telling you to *write it down* and/or draw in your box, then come back here and do it.

I'll leave you some room to write and, as always, a box for you to draw in.

_____

_____

_____

_____

_____

_____

_____

_____

_____

CHAPTER 12

I Am Redeemed

Before I could truly let go of the record of wrongs nugget, I had a letter and a video to send. I had a revelation through prayer—that I was not the only one that had suffered a great deal over the past few years. The Lord showed me every tiny detail of my wrongs, and He told me to apologize.

For the first time throughout this journey, I didn't argue with God. In fact, I so willingly did it. He told me to send Tyler a video, apologizing, and that's exactly what I did. God helped me see that if I trusted Him, then I must trust Tyler. I wasn't afraid Tyler would use the video against me. I wasn't embarrassed or too prideful. I wasn't ashamed, and I wasn't worried about him showing anyone.

Without fear, I trusted. I just simply trusted! So that night after praying for Tyler for what seemed like hours, I got in my closet, sat on the floor, cried my eyes out, and made a video apologizing to the man that the enemy had been using to wreck my world. And I did it with complete sincerity and humbleness. I was truly sorrowful with a godly sorrow, yet redeemed, peaceful, and joyful. I had true love in my heart. I was living proof that out of the abundance of the heart, the mouth speaks.

Read Luke 6:45.

If I had told you that only five days prior to sending that video, I had been served divorce papers, that not only had false allegations and information in them but also said he requested temporary relief, before I told you about the apology, would you have been as accepting of God and I deciding an apology to him was the way to go? If you said no, I don't blame you. I would have told you how crazy you are if the roles were reversed.

But here's the thing—I had already began to see the work of the Father when just two days after I received the papers, and three days before I made the video, I sent pictures to Tyler of a letter I had handwritten him. I had gone two weeks without talking or texting him at all because Proverbs 17:28 says even a fool, when he keeps silent, is considered wise. When he closes his lips, he is considered prudent. And Proverbs 10:19 says when there are many words, transgression is unavoidable, but he who restrains his lips is wise.

Because I knew my words wouldn't have been few, I used wisdom and kept silent. The letter was the first thing I said to him, although it wasn't the first for him to say to me. But this time it was different. His response to my letter was actually kind, and y'all, that was God and *only* God.

I saw the first glimpse of the work God had promised me He would do only two days after I received divorce papers. It may have only been a tiny glimpse, but I saw it.

TAKE THAT, SATAN! (Insert the fist emoji in your mind.)

Something was beginning to change, and I rejoiced in truth. I didn't let Satan steal the truth from me this time. My faith grew, and my belief was strong. So when it came time for the video, I trusted!

Here's a copy of the letter

Dear Tyler (the love of my life),
    Because of my undying love for you, I have
made it known, that I am willing to grant you a

divorce. Not because I want to, but because I do not want to deny you the life you want.

I asked for the time from the beginning, so that I could gain wisdom from God, before proceeding. I knew I needed to continue this process through the spirit, and not my feelings. Why, because my feelings are all over the place. As a human being, that is in love, naturally, my own feelings say many different things, so I didn't want to do this in my own feelings and cause this to go any other way than God's perfect will, and through 100% godly love for you, instead of my human love for you.

In my flesh, I have wanted to beg and fight for you, but the Holy Spirit teaches me to remain silent instead of arguing.

In my flesh, I have wanted to feel offended and angry, but God continues to teach what love truly is. God has corrected my ways and my thoughts more times than I can count, and through that, I have grown to love you even more than I thought possible. I have learned to love you the way He teaches us to love. I know that must be very hard for you to see because I have made mistakes along the way, but believe me when I say, even when we don't see it, He's working. With all of that said, through it all, I have not only thought of myself, I have thought of you, and most of all, our baby boys. I've seeked God's counsel for all of us. I've held tight to our marriage license so that I could be sure to honor those vows in the good times, and now, the bad. I have prayed more than I've ever prayed before, not just for our marriage, but for me to become a better woman in Him, and for the divorce.

As I sit here, looking at the license, that granted our union in marriage, sitting on top of the papers, with intent to end that very union, I still want to honor the vows, I made, all those years ago. I said I would love you in the bad times, so let me do that. I'm asking you, once again, to do this the best way for us all. Not because I want to prolong it, but because I don't want to prolong, and because I don't want there to be a winner and a loser. I don't want to have to use a record of wrongs and repay evil for evil. I don't want our boys, drug through the mud, anymore, than they already have been. I want their relationship with you to be rebuilt, not torn down even more.

While I hate with everything in me, to give up the fight, to be one, with you, my intentions are not to keep you from leaving, they are to keep you from leaving, the wrong way. I cannot make this decision for you, I realize that, so this has never been, and is not for control purposes, it's 100% love. I have always loved you no matter what, and I always will, so now it's up to you, before I proceed and respond through a lawyer, to your complaint for divorce. I'm asking, one more time, to do it the right way. If you say proceed the way it is now, then my back will be against the wall, and it will kill me to do it this way, but I will. I don't want to control the situation, I want you to know, that you know, that you know, that I am trying to be good to you, no matter what, and doing it the way you're asking for it to be done, through these papers, will cause so much more unnecessary harm to everyone. If you choose to go another route, I can send you some information.

Dear Tyler (the love of my life),

Because of my undying love for you, I have made it known, that I am willing to grant you a divorce. Not because I want to, but because I do not want to deny you, the life you want.

I asked for time from the beginning so that I could gain wisdom from God before proceeding. I knew I needed to continue this process through the Spirit and not my feelings. Why? Because my feelings are all over the place. As a human being, that is in love, naturally my own feelings say many different things, so I didn't want to do this in my own feelings and cause this to go any other way than God's perfect will and through 100% Godly love for you, instead of my human love for you.

In my flesh, I have wanted to beg and fight for you, but the Holy Spirit teaches me to remain silent, instead of arguing.

In my flesh, I have wanted to feel offended and angry, but

God continues to teach what love truly is. God has corrected my ways and my thoughts more times than I can count. and through that, I have grown to love you even more than I thought possible. I have learned to love you the way he teaches us to love. I know that must be very hard for you to see because I have made mistakes along the way, but believe me when I say, even when we don't see it, He's working. With all of that said, through it all I have not only thought of myself, I have thought of you, and most of all, our baby boys. I've seeked God's counsel for all of us. I've held tight to our marriage license so that I could be sure I honored those vows in the good times and now the bad. I have prayed more than I've ever prayed before, not just for our marriage, but for me to become a better woman in him,

and for the divorce.
As I sit here looking at the
license that granted our union
in marriage, sitting on top of
the papers with intent to end
that very union; I still want
to honor the vows I made all
those years ago. I said I would
love you in the bad times, so let
me do that. I'm asking you
once again to do this the best
way for us all. Not because I
want to prolong it, but because
I don't want to prolong it, and
because I don't want there to
be a winner and a loser. I don't
want to have to use a record of
wrongs and repay evil for evil. I
don't want our boys drug through
the mud anymore than they have
been. I want their relationship
with you to be rebuilt, not torn
down even more.
   While I hate with everything
in me to give up the fight to be
one with you, my intentions are
not, to keep you from leaving,

they are to keep you from leaving the wrong way. I cannot make this decision for you, I realize that, so this has never been and is not for control purposes, It's 100% LOVE. I have always loved you (no matter what) and I always will. So now it's up to you, before I proceed and respond, through a lawyer, to your complaint for divorce; I'm asking one more time to do it the right way. If you say proceed the way it is now, then my back will be against the wall and it will kill me to do it this way, but I will. I don't want to control this situation, I want you to know that you know, that you know, that I am trying to be good to you no matter what, and doing it the way you're asking it to be done, through these papers, will cause so much more unnecessary harm to everyone. If you choose to go another route, I can send you some information.

I had no shame or pride. I laid it all out there!

Wanna see the video I sent him? Go to Bitty from Ashes (YouTube channel) and watch "The Apology."

Just as I thought the journey was complete, I remembered there were five nuggets and I was on number four. I had one to go!

Before we move on to the next chapter, look up a scripture for me and write it below.

Proverbs 14:11

_____

_____

_____

CHAPTER 13

House or Tent

Have you ever visited a battlefield? If so, stop for a minute and think about it. What are some of the things you saw, and how did it impact you? Did you try to put yourself in the shoes of the soldiers that fought in the battle? Think deeply with me for a minute. Can you actually imagine what they went through? No, you can't!

No matter how much we try, we will never fully understand what they went through. We will never be able to smell the gunpowder. It was their battle to fight, so the deep details of it can only be fully understood by the soldiers who fought in it and God. It's the exact same way for us as Christian soldiers in a battle. You will never fully know all of the details of the war I fought and you'll never be able to smell the gunpowder, but I'm more than willing to bet you have or will fight a battle of your own. Just like me, you have parts of the war that only you and God can fully understand, but there is one thing that will be the same—God never loses a battle!

As my battle comes to an end, watch how God crushed the enemy and won the war. You have no idea how much and how loudly I'm shouting right now! Chills are all up and down my spine. OUR GOD IS SO FAITHFUL!

Like it was yesterday, I remember sitting at the dining room table with my parents, listening while they tried to protect their little girl and grandsons. Like any parents would, they continually told me I needed to keep the house. Tears began rolling down my face. It was as though my hand couldn't even grip the pen that was supposed to write my future without Tyler in it on paper.

Like you, my parents only knew what I could tell them. They couldn't hear what the Lord was telling me. It was my battle to face and God's war to win. This may seem like strength to you, like I was so strong in my faith that I knew God would fix it before it came to that point, but that wasn't the case.

Although I trusted in the Lord with every part of my being, and I knew he had my marriage in His hands, I still didn't know exactly when or how it would all take place. I was well aware that I had to continue on, letting Tyler proceed with the divorce, and I had to plan the future for myself and the boys. But in that exact moment, I couldn't write because I felt no peace.

Anything I had before felt that we deserved and needed just didn't feel right to take, but I couldn't put my finger on what that feeling meant until my mother's next words. She looked at me in a way that I had never seen her look. I could tell it pained her to ask it because after all what parent would actually want this for their child? And I'm pretty sure it must have been a battle she was facing of her own, but she asked this, "What do you want to do, Bitty, give it all to him? Would it bring you peace to just give it all to Tyler?"

I didn't have to think for more than half a second. That thought stopped everything in its tracks. No more tears, no more turmoil, and no more anxiety! The room was suddenly calm. My mind that just seconds before was spinning out of control was now at complete and utter peace. A half smile came to my face as I looked at my mom and said, "Yes, ma'am. I feel more peace right now than I have felt throughout this entire process." I'm sure my parents had a hard time accepting it, but they supported me in my decision, not because they trusted me but because they trust God.

Even though you can't smell the gunpowder of that battle, I hope you can feel at least a tiny bit of the peace I felt while we go back and look again at the scripture I had you look up at the end of the last chapter. Read it again now please. Proverbs 14:11.

This is yet another example of how good our God is and how He goes before us. Just the day before, this scripture was one I had read, and it came straight to my mind as I sat at my dining room table when peace entered.

Even if I had given up the house we lived in for sixteen years and everything I owned, I had nothing to fear. I only stood to gain because I was showing mercy and submitting to the will of my husband. In return, all I wanted was the peace of having a closer walk with God. I was flourishing—growing in grace and in good works. Even if I ended up living in a cardboard box, I was sure that my new home would be even better than I could've imagined because my eyes were ultimately set on my *true fortress* and my *eternal* dwelling place.

The next couple of days were so good. I actually did something that I hadn't done in a few months. I laughed and had a good time. I had finally let go and let God take control. I allowed Him to be my fortress. I stopped having to be quiet because I was able to use words of wisdom without fear I would mess up. I was kind because it came naturally. Then it happened. It was gone. My fifth nugget was gone. But I had not even noticed yet.

Let's pause for a minute.

Do me a favor and tell Alexa, or your music source of choice, to play "Oceans" by Hillsong United and listen to it with intent.

Even if you're like me and you've already heard it a thousand times, close your eyes and listen intently. Please don't read any further until you're done with the song.

Now that you've listened, let your doodling time and space be for writing/doodling the following.

"Spirit lead me where my trust is without Borders"

While you're doodling, think about how far God can lead you if you truly mean you want no borders. You can make it as cute as you want, but continue doodling it until you know God is done speaking to you about trusting Him.

After you have committed to trust God without borders, think on this.

Those are the exact words I doodled on my driveway with sidewalk chalk, the day before the Holy Spirit led me into peace over giving Tyler everything *we* owned with no strings attached.

CHAPTER 14

—∿—

Godly Desires from a Journey That's Complete

I think you've seen enough of my journal by now to know that God and I have real conversations. He desires to converse with all of His children. I cannot imagine a one-sided conversation with my own children turning out very well, so why do we think that's how our Heavenly Father wants it to be? He desires to hear from us, but He equally desires for us to hear from Him. Sit often in God's presence and listen with all of your heart.

This is what He said to me, just before a miracle happened.

April 22, 2020

My Conversation with God

ME. God, you know my options.

Before I could say anything else, God spoke.

GOD. You know what to do.

ME. Yes, Lord, and I'm sorry for not trusting the way I should. It's me, I don't trust, not you.

GOD. You know my voice.

ME. But I don't hear it audibly, and that makes it hard.

GOD. Write it all down. Write down all the things I've done for you so that you don't doubt my existence and my voice.

GOD. SEEK FIRST THE KINGDOM OF GOD!

Be still and know that I am God!

I told you it's through the cleanliness of your hands that Tyler will be brought back to me.

It's through your submission, meekness, and quietness that a man can be shown God.

I told you to cover your ears to what the world says you should do and close your mouth, through Linda.

I told you to dwell on me and not the things that drag you to the ground, through Troy and your pastor.

I told you to keep a sweet spirit, through your pastor.

You heard me and look what happened with women you helped. You were brought peace, and through you, they have peace.

Through Krystal, I confirmed what you already heard me say, "Write it down," on April 10, 2020.

I told you who you are, through Shanna.

You heard me say paint what love is and look where it has brought you. Love is not only for others, it's for yourself. Stop keeping a record of wrongs for yourself. I'm showing you what love is not and what it is so that you will give love to others but also to receive it from others. Give love to yourself. I have done a work in you, trust me enough to trust yourself. I trust you.

You can do it. This is your reward.

You burned an offering to me.

You saw your brother, and I spoke through him.

You slayed a giant.

You learned that the love of money is truly the root of all evil (possessions too) and you gave them up, for peace.

How many times have I brought peace before you?

Your brother!

Do you think you named your son? No, I did. I filled him, while he was still in your womb, and I named him. He is peace!

I have used my other son to hold you and care for you in your darkest hours. Yes, he is my son. Not yours. He's mine, trust me with him.

I sent Gay Lynn to tell you, you need peace, and I told her to tell you about a book, then Cindy to send it to you.

I sent a sermon, through Cindy, exactly when you needed it. And through Cindy, I sent the drawing, of me holding your hand.

Cindy is my faithful servant.

Don't forget the peaceful walks we've taken together.

The mother and father I gave you, are not by chance. They have never left you. They have been by your side, the whole time.

Remember the message, I had you record, on TV, to ease your anxious mind.

Look at the record of wrongs you deleted, in trust.

You know who you are.

You accomplished it!

You threw those nuggets to the dust and you are free of all that has bound you.

Your chains have fallen.

I have rewarded you!

Now let me finish setting you free.

You no longer worry what others think of you, you look for my approval only. You want only to show others who I am through you. You don't feel the need to argue who you are. I have rewarded you with wisdom.

You protected him, to Keila.

You have defeated your fear of Satan. I did not give you a spirit of fear.

I told you to write...forgiven, listen, and love.

You are there, you have been forgiven and you have given forgiveness. You are listening to my voice, and you have learned to

love enough that you are willing to forgive those who have wronged you, as far as the east is from the west.
Your anger turned to silence.
Great is your reward.
You rejoice in truth.
You have sought my kingdom first, you have delighted yourself in me, now tell me the desires of your heart.

ME. To be pleasing to you.
To bring others to know you.
Your perfect will to be done.
For Tyler to fall so in love with you.
And for my marriage to be completely restored and even better than it's ever been.
And for more wisdom.
For my storm to calm, and have life *abundantly.*

Friendships have been restored. I am willing to do God's work. I have overcome my fear of a job. I have realized the value of a marriage and family, including Suzie and Fufi. I have watched both of my sons step up. Ty Majer has spoken at church and FCA. Mason has taught me lots of things. Angela and I were restored through this. I turned down offers from men. I have learned to love, even when I don't get love in return.

Then I rated myself on how well I loved according to 1 Corinthians 13:1 again. These ratings are in chapter 11, on the journal entry page called "Ask Myself, Do I Love?"

4-22-20
My conversation with God...
me... God you know my options
Before I could say anything
else

God... You know what to do.
me... Yes Lord, & I'm sorry for not
trusting the way I should.
It's me I don't trust, not you.
God... You know my voice.
me... But I don't audibly hear
It & that makes it hard.
God... write it all down. write
down all the things I've done
for you so that you don't
doubt my existence & my
voice.

SEEK FIRST THE KINGDOM OF
GOD!

Be still & know that I am God!

I told you, its through the
cleanliness of your hands that he
will be brought back to me.

* It's through your submission, meekness & quietness that a man can be shown God.

* I told you to cover your ears & shut your mouth through Linda

* I told you to dwell on me & not ~~your~~ the things that drug you to the ground through Thoy & your pastor

* I told you to keep a sweet spirit through your pastor

* You heard me & look what happened w/ megan, look what happened w/ Raven. You were brought peace & through you, they have peace.

* Through Krystal I confirmed what you already heard me say "Write It down" on 4-10-20

* I told you, who you are through Shanna.
* You heard me say paint what love is, and look where it has brought you

— Love is not only for others, its for yourself! Stop keeping a record of wrongs for yourself. I'm showing you what love is not & what it is so that you will give love to others but also to receive it from others. Give love to yourself.
I have done a work in you, trust me enough to trust yourself. I trust you You can do it. This is your reward.

* You burned an offering to me
* You saw your brother & I spoke through him
* You slayed a giant
* You learned that the love of money is truly the root of all evil (posessions too) & you gave them up for peace.

How many times have I brought
peace before you?
-Your brother
-Do you think you named your
son? No... I did. I filled him
while he was in your womb &
I named him. HE IS PEACE
- I have used my other son
to hold you & care for you
in your darkest hours. Yet he's
my son. Not yours. He's mine,
trust me with him.
- I sent Gay Lynn to tell you,
you need peace & I told her
to tell you about a book, then
Cindy to send it to you.
- I sent a sermon through
Cindy exactly when you
needed it. And through Cindy
I sent the drawing of me
holding your hand Cindy's my
faithful servant.
- Don't forget the peaceful
walks we've taken together.

* The mother & father I gave you, are not
* by chance. They have never left you.
~~They have been by~~ your side the whole time.
— Remember the messages I had
you record on TV to ease your
anxious mind.

* Look @ the record of wrongs
you deleted in trust.
* You know who you are
You accomplished it!
You threw those nuggets to
the dust & you are free of
all that has bound you.
* Your chains have fallen.
I have rewarded you!!!
Now let me finish setting you
free.
* You no longer "worry" what
others think of you, you
look for my approval only.
You want only to show
others who I am through
you. You don't feel the need to
argue who you are. I have
rewarded you with wisdom.
* You protected him to Keila

* You have defeated your fear of
Satan. I did not give you a spirit of
fear.
* I told you to write ...

FORGIVEN
LISTEN
LOVE

You are there, you have been
forgiven & you have given
forgiveness. You are listening to
my voice, and you have learned
to love enough that you are
willing to forgive those who
have wronged you & as far as
the east is from the west.
* Your anger turned to silence
* Great is your reward
* You rejoice in truth
* You have seeked my kingdom
first, you have delighted
yourself in me, now tell
me the desires of your
heart.
   -to be pleasing to you
   - to bring others to know you
   - your perfect will to be done
   - for Tyler to fall so in love
   with you

— & for my marriage to be
completely restored & even
better than it's ever been
— & for more wisdom
— for my storm to calm & have
life abundantly

*Friendships have been restored
* I am willing to do God's work
* I have overcome my fear of
a job
* I have realized the value of
a marriage & family. Including
Suzie & Fuh
* I have watched both of my
sons step & up. Th has
spoken @ church & FCA
Mason has taught me lots of
things
* Angela & me were restored
through this
* I turned down offers from men
* I have learned to love enou even
when I don't get it in return

4-20-20 <u>Maror gave me this</u>
David did not use the
armor he was told that
he needed b/c he trusted
& knew he only needed
what God told him.
I do not need this
evidence.

I deleted all evidence in
trust. I trust you Lord!!!

Focus on the last thing God said to me for just a moment, and let's break it into two parts.

Part 1: "You have sought my kingdom first, and you have delighted yourself in me."

It was in that moment that I finally realized my chains were gone. I had been set free!

Nuggets of Gold

1. Pride
2. Impure possessions
3. Money
4. Record of wrongs
5. Control

I had given it all to God. I had assigned all of my nuggets of gold to the dust because I had completed a journey of trusting my creator, my Lord. I learned to seek His kingdom and His righteousness first, and because of that, I delighted myself in Him.

Because I delighted myself in the Lord, the desires of my heart changed so He knew I was ready.

Part 2: "Now tell me the desires of your heart."

For the first time, I felt a "well done my good and faithful servant" feeling all over me. Did you read that with power? In case you missed just how big that is, let me take a minute to explain it a little more in-depth.

First, let's look up the word *delight*. Write it below.
Delight

_____

_____

_____

Let's never get confused by Scripture because of our lack of knowledge in vocabulary and/or lack of focus on each word.

How can we possibly have desires of the heart that don't line up with the word of God and His will for our lives if we are delighting—greatly pleasing, giving joy—to our Heavenly Father?

If we are pleasing Him greatly, the desires of our hearts are different than they were when we were lukewarm, so it goes hand in hand. He will give you your desires because they will be the same as His desires. They will be desires that will give you life that you can live abundantly.

Here's a scripture challenge that is a little different than I've been giving.

I referenced two scriptures in the last paragraph. For some of you, it will be easy to see them. I'm sure some of you probably even know the exact book, chapter, and verse. But for others, it might take some digging. For growth purposes, will you take the time to pick them out, find them in the Bible, and write the scripture of each?

_____

_____

_____

_____

_____

_____

If you did it and you've never done that before, I hope you were able to see that it wasn't that hard. Studying God's word is a joy that is unspeakable and so worth the time.

Tyler got off the rig on April 29, 2020, and, one day later, showed up at our house once again without warning. And this time, it was before seven in the morning. I opened my eyes to him standing in our bedroom, digging through dresser drawers, but I wasn't scared of him this time. My eyes opened peacefully, and I simply said, "Hey, Ty."

Try to smell that gunpowder!

My Desires

To be pleasing to you.
  To bring others to know you.
  Your perfect will to be done.
  For Tyler to fall so in love with you.
  For my marriage to be completely restored,
and even better, than it's ever been.
  For more wisdom.
  For my storm to calm, and have life
abundantly.

Why did I say, "Listen with all of your heart," in the last sentence of the first paragraph in this chapter when I suggested that you sit often in God's presence and listen with all of your heart?

Read Proverbs 3:5–6 and write it below.

_____

_____

_____

_____

_____

_____

Highlight the words *trust, heart,* and *lean not on your own understanding.*

Understanding comes from the mind. Our minds are all over the place, changing often. Our hearts, on the other hand, can't be changed so quickly and easily. The heart thinks on its own and sends messages to the brain. It's very capable of telling the mind what to do. This is why the Lord wants our heart, not just our mind.

How about you, what are your desires?

_____

_____

_____

_____

_____

_____

_____

_____

Look back at this in three to six months and see what God has done for you since you first wrote it.

CHAPTER 15

My Son's Come Home Again

The need for control is a dangerous thing. To give up all control and surrender to God is not scary when you *know* the peace speaker.

The voice I heard respond and the eyes I saw look at me when I said, "Hey Ty," to my Tyler, was almost just that—the voice and the eyes of the man I knew long ago. He saw an angel (his words, not mine), and I saw how God had been working even when I didn't know it.

Tyler left our bedroom to give Mason the birthday gift he had opted out of giving him five weeks earlier then returned to our room to be given the news. This was what I said, "I know you're going to your lawyer today to write up the new papers. Before you go, I want you know, it's yours, Ty. You can have it all. You've worked hard for what we have, and I don't desire to take any of it from you. If there's anything left that you don't want, you can give it to me, if that's what you want. You can give me what you think I deserve, but please only give me what you don't want. I am still your wife, and I will be submissive to you until the day I am not, so I want your desires over mine. I know the Lord will provide all of my needs. I truly want you to be happy, and that's it. I just want God."

I saw tears fill his eyes, and a love like I had not felt in a very long time filled our bedroom. But before his mouth could open to speak, I saw the enemy intervene, and Tyler left.

Did I say all of that to him because I felt undeserving? No, not at all. Don't forget chapter 13 when peace entered my whole body, mind, heart, soul, and spirit.

I said it because I meant it. I said it because I had changed. I said it because I no longer needed control. I said it because I trusted. I said it because my chains were gone. And I said it because I knew God.

Look up Philippians 2:3 and write it please.

_____

_____

_____

That speaks for itself.

Look up and write, one more for me.
Proverbs 14:1

_____

_____

_____

I had been foolish in the past and had torn my home apart with my own hands, but I was no longer willing to be foolish. I was determined to build my house, even if…

If you begin to see things in your spouse that you've never seen in a negative way before, do yourself a favor and consider that you might not be *seeing* at all. It could very possibly be that you're going blind. Spiritual blindness causes a foolishness that will tear your home down! Matthew 16:19 (NIV) says, "I will give you the keys of the kingdom of heaven; whatever you bind on earth will be bound in heaven, and whatever you loose on earth will be loosed in heaven." Take those keys, or authority, bind up the spirit of blindness, and let loose the power, love, and self-control that is given to you through the Holy Spirit so that you can *see*. Choose to use wisdom and build your house.

As soon as Tyler left, I called my mama to tell her what happened and to ask her to pray. Then I began to pray myself. I knew where he was going, but I also knew I saw a little bit of a change in him. When I got off of my knees and began to praise God through worship, God said, *"Fight!"* He put a fire inside of me, and I began to fight battles through praise. I didn't know exactly what the battles were, but God did!

You've waited long enough, now you finally get to see the miracle unfold in a way that only the God of Abraham, Isaac, and Jacob, the God of you, and the God of me, can perform. He is the one and only true king. He's God of the impossible.

Tyler had driven to his appointment with the lawyer, only to get there to a locked door. For no reason at all, with no phone call to reschedule and not even a note on the door, his lawyer wasn't there. She nor her secretary would answer their phones. If you've ever had to use an attorney for anything, you know, *that does not happen!*

Tyler was not a happy camper, or at least the darkness that hovered over him, the one that was losing the battle, wasn't. After a few choice words, he angrily headed back to our house. When he arrived, he found me outside, praying and reading the journal I had been writing in, and he sat beside me in complete silence. He listened to me pray, and he listened to the worship music I had playing without running off. The Lord prompted me to begin reading my journal aloud, so I did without stopping.

I could see God working one minute and the enemy well up in Tyler the very next, but I never stopped reading and Tyler never stopped listening. It was war, and I could physically and spiritually see the battle. This went on for hours.

When I thought the enemy was about to win, out of pure exhaustion, I gave in and said, "I give up. I want all of this back-and-forth mess to end. I want this divorce to be done." I had gone as far as I could go. I had no more fight left in me. I took off my gloves. I was about to award Satan the champion belt when God stepped in one final time. And with the hardest blow yet, He knocked Satan to the ground for the countdown.

Ten, nine, eight, seven, six, five, four, three, two, one—Satan never got back on his feet. God won! Remember, He has never lost a battle, and He never will! God's son, Tyler Patrick McCraw, ran to the mercy seat and came home again right then. I could just hear the angels rejoicing as Tyler turned to me that evening and said, "Are you sure that's what you want? Because I don't. I thought I did, but I've been blind. I can see now!"

I could see and feel the amazement and shock all over him. He was both well-informed and confused at the same time. He couldn't believe who he had been. After letting him know that was absolutely not what I wanted either, his next words were my favorite, and I'll never forget them. He said, "How can you ever forgive me and how can you possibly still love me after all I've done?"

With a loving smile and a deep look into his eyes, I said, "Love is patient, love is kind. It does not envy, it does not boast, it is not proud. It does not dishonor others, it is not self-seeking, it is not easily angered, it keeps no record of wrongs. Love does not delight in evil but rejoices with truth. It always protects, always trusts, always hopes, and always perseveres. Love never fails." *Then I washed his feet*!

Tyler got on his knees and gave his life back to God that very night, and he has proven day in and day out that he gave his heart back to me and our boys every day since.

I was a thirty-seven-year-old woman when I got my miracle on April 30, 2020. Tyler and I renewed our vows on June 6, 2020.

Go back once more to the desires of my heart in chapter 14 and put a check mark beside all that have been fulfilled.

GOD IS TRULY A GOOD FATHER! Delight yourself in the Lord, and He will give you the desires of your heart (Psalm 37:4 NIV).

You say I am loved
when I can't feel a thing
You say I am strong
when I think I am weak
You say I am held
when I am falling short
and when I don't belong
You say I am Yours.
And I believe
Yes, I believe
what You say of me.
I BELIEVE!

Go to YouTube one last time and listen to "You Say." That's my mom and I singing in my bathroom, April 24, 2020. That's just six days before I got my miracle. That miracle, I assured my mom I would get over and over again.

Who Are You?

_____

_____

_____

_____

_____

_____

_____

_____

_____

_____

_____

_____

_____

_____

_____

_____

_____

_____

_____

_____

_____

_____

_____

_____

_____

_____

Go back to the beginning and read who you were back then. Read 1 Corinthians 13 one last time. After reading it, go back to the rating page in chapter 2 and rate yourself again.

This is not the end. This is only the beginning!

IN THE CHANCERY COURT OF CLARKE COUNTY
THE STATE OF MISSISSIPPI

TYLER MCCRAW   PLAINTIFF

VS.   Case No. 20-0062-S

DONIELLE MCCRAW   DEFENDANT

NOTICE OF DISMISSAL

Pursuant to Rule 41(a)(1) of the Mississippi Rules of Civil Procedure, the Plaintiff, Tyler McCraw, wishes to dismiss the previously filed Complaint for Divorce (MEC doc. #1) and his Amended Complaint for Divorce (MEC doc. #5) without prejudice.

The Defendant has not filed an answer or a motion for summary judgment.

THIS THE ____1____ day of May, 2020.

Respectfully submitted,

Tyler McCraw,
Plaintiff

BY: */s/: Frances Smith Stephenson, MSB #101710*
His Attorney

Stephenson Law Offices, PLLC
Post Office Box 5673
Meridian, MS 39302
(601) 693-2246 (telephone)
(601) 693-2268 (facsimile)
stephensonfs@bellsouth.net

About the Author

—ɷ—

Donielle McCraw—nicknamed Bitty by her dad, who nicknames everyone he likes, for her small size as a child—has been known by this nickname most of her life. She's a small-town woman from Enterprise, Mississippi, who remains true to her southern roots.

She holds her relationship with God, family, and those walking through fire above all else. She's happily the wife to one husband—her favorite person in the world, Tyler—and mother to their two sons, Mason and Ty Majer.

Second to being a wife and mother, she's an interior designer and decorator that, together with her husband, owns Without Borders where she designs and Tyler (the builder) makes it happen.

She is simply a willing vessel for the work of the Lord who wants nothing more or less than to answer the call of God. She has been through many struggles and trials throughout her life but is happy to be able to stand today to give her testimony through them all.

She humbly takes pride in being a normal woman without perfection, needing the help of the Lord to make it through each day of the battles of balancing womanly duties. Her deepest desire is to see the promises of God fulfilled and the lies and tricks of Satan put to death while he loses each battle. She can't wait to see the army of men, women, and marriages rise up from ashes.

CPSIA information can be obtained
at www.ICGtesting.com
Printed in the USA
BVHW021531210222
629674BV00018B/629